Learning How to Fly

Born on 15 October 1931, at Rameswaram in Tamil Nadu, **Dr Avul Pakir Jainulabdeen Abdul Kalam** specialized in Aeronautical Engineering from Madras Institute of Technology. Dr Kalam was a distinguished scientist and was awarded the Padma Bhushan (1981), the Padma Vibhushan (1990) and India's highest civilian award, the Bharat Ratna (1997).

Dr Kalam became the eleventh President of India on 25 July 2002. His focus and greatest ambition was finding ways to transform India into a developed nation.

Other books by A.P.J. Abdul Kalam (from Rupa Publications)

My Journey: Transforming Dreams Into Action
The Righteous Life: The Very Best of A.P.J. Abdul Kalam
Governance for Growth in India
The Guiding Light: A Selection of Quotations from My Favourite Books
My Life: An Illustrated Autobiography

A.P.J. ABDUL KALAM

Learning How to Fly

LIFE LESSONS FOR THE YOUTH

RUPA

Published by
Rupa Publications India Pvt. Ltd 2016
7/16, Ansari Road, Daryaganj
New Delhi 110002

Sales centres:
Allahabad Bengaluru Chennai
Hyderabad Jaipur Kathmandu
Kolkata Mumbai

ISBN: 978-81-291-4215-3

Nineteenth impression 2021

25 24 23 22 21 20 19

The moral right of the author has been asserted.

Printed at Thomson Press India Ltd., Faridabad

Contents

Publisher's Note

Dr A.P.J. Abdul Kalam did many things in his life—he was a scientist, a leader, the President of India and a teacher. Of all these roles, the one that gave him the greatest joy was that of a teacher. For him, there was nothing as important as talking to the youth and telling them about the world of opportunities that awaited them if they pursued the right kind of knowledge. He spent much of his time in the years after he had completed his term as President, travelling all over the country, meeting students, interacting with them, talking to them and listening to them.

The lectures that he gave at these interactions distilled the thoughts behind what he felt was important for the young. He spoke about the concept of the 'ignited mind'. A mind that has been exposed to the highest thought processes, sources of inspiration, been told about the great inventions and discoveries of the world and how the greatest men and women achieved their greatness, is a mind that has been ignited by the light of knowledge.

In this book, some of his best, most detailed and interesting lectures addressed to the youth in various parts of the country have been collected. These lectures were given to school students, college students, those studying in professional colleges like engineering or medicine, and even to students outside the country. Also included here are lectures that he gave to teachers, librarians and caregivers of children.

From these lectures, what emerges is a mind that was forever thirsty for knowledge, almost childlike in its curiosity about new studies and discoveries, and a mind that thought and felt deeply about the challenges the youth face today and the ways in which they can overcome them. He delivered a deeply optimistic lesson about believing in oneself and developing confidence to become future leaders. He firmly believed that 'The problem should not be the master. Take charge and become the master of the problem.'

These lectures make for fascinating reading that will take the youth through key episodes of Dr Kalam's life, his inspirations and the stories of his mentors. They will also help them understand the challenges the country faces and the best ways in which they can make a truly compassionate, equal and great society.

Learning How to Fly will tell every reader, in Dr Kalam's own words, that each of us have wings and that we are capable of flying high.

I Will Fly

I am born with wings
So, I am not meant for crawling,
I have wings, I will fly.

Dear students and teachers, I would like to share few thoughts on how to achieve the goals in life. There are some proven steps:

- Finding an aim in life before you are twenty years old;
- Acquire knowledge continuously to reach this goal;
- Work hard and persevere so you can defeat all the problems and succeed.

There is a famous verse 'I will fly' by the thirteenth-century Persian Sufi poet Jalaluddin Rumi:

I will fly

I am born with potential
I am born with goodness and trust
I am born with ideas and dreams
I am born with greatness
I am born with confidence
I am born with wings
So, I am not meant for crawling,
I have wings, I will fly
I will fly and fly.

Young friends, education is the instrument that gives you wings to fly. Only when your subconscious mind says 'I will win' and you believe you can reach your goal, does it become a reality. Each one of you assembled here and elsewhere, have wings of fire. The wings of fire lead to knowledge which will make you fly as doctors, or engineers, or scientists, or teachers, or political leaders, or bureaucrats or diplomats. Or you could walk on the moon and Mars or do anything else you may want to.

When we see electric bulbs, immediately our thoughts go to the inventor Thomas Alva Edison. He invented the electric bulb and electrical lighting system.

When we hear the sound of aeroplanes flying overhead whom do you think of? The Wright brothers proved that man could fly.

Whom does the telephone remind you of? Alexander Graham Bell.

When people all over the world considered sea travel only as an experience or a voyage, one person during his sea travel from United Kingdom to India started pondering why the horizon where the sky and sea meet looked blue. His research resulted in the discovery of the phenomena of scattering of light. For this, Sir C.V. Raman was awarded the Nobel Prize.

There was an Indian mathematician who did not have formal higher education but had an inexhaustible spirit and love for mathematics. This took him on a path where he ended up contributing to the treasure houses of mathematical research—some of which are still under serious study and engaging mathematicians' efforts all over the world to establish formal proofs. He was a genius who melted the heart of the most hardened and outstanding Cambridge mathematician Professor G.H. Hardy. In fact, it is not an exaggeration to say that it was Professor Hardy who discovered a great mathematician in number theory Srinivasa Ramanujan and brought his genius to the world.

All these people were thirsty for knowledge and their works and names are now immortal.

I have met 21.5 million youth in a decade's time. From these meetings and interactions such as this one, I learnt that every youth wants to be unique. You can only be YOU! But the world all around you is doing its best, day and night, to make you just like everybody else. At home, you are asked by your parents to be like the neighbours' children and score good marks like them. When you go to school, your teachers say, 'Why can't you be among the top five in the class?' Wherever you go, they are saying, 'You have to be somebody else or like everybody else.' But young friends, I know that all of you would like to be the unique yourself.

The challenge, my young friends, is that you have to fight the hardest battle, and never stop fighting until you arrive at your destined place. What will be the tools with which you will fight this battle? They are: have a great aim in life, continuously acquire the knowledge, work hard and persevere to realize the great achievement.

During your studies in your schools you will acquire a great friend who will accompany you forever. Who is that friend? That friend is knowledge. I am giving you here the knowledge equation:

Knowledge = Creativity + Righteousness + Courage

Let's take each of these parts one by one.

Creativity
Learning gives creativity,
Creativity leads to thinking,
Thinking provides knowledge,
Knowledge makes you great.

The next component of knowledge is righteousness. This aspect can be described in a divine hymn.

Righteousness
Where there is righteousness in the heart,
There is beauty in the character.
When there is beauty in the character,
there is harmony in the home.
When there is harmony in the home,
There is an order in the nation.
When there is order in the nation,
There is peace in the world.

Now the question is: How do we inculcate righteousness in the heart? In my opinion, there are three sources which can bring righteousness in the heart of the youth. They are mother, father and, the third and the most important is, the teacher, particularly the primary school teacher.

The third component is courage, which is defined as follows:

Courage
Courage to think differently,
Courage to invent,
Courage to travel into an unexplored path,
Courage to discover the impossible,
Courage to combat the problems and succeed,
are the unique qualities of the youth.
As a youth of my nation, I will work and work
with courage to achieve success in all the missions.

Where will knowledge come from? Knowledge can be found at home, in good books, from teachers and from an enriching, learning environment. It can be acquired by coming into contact with good human beings. When schools teach students to use the knowledge they impart with creativity, righteousness and courage, it will result in the nation having a large number of empowered and enlightened citizens. This in turn is vital for the growth of the individual, growth of the family, growth of nation and promotion of peace in the world.

In the present situation in the world where every citizen wants to live in a prosperous and peaceful atmosphere, the empowerment of youth with enlightenment becomes vital. This has three dimensions which are:

- Education with a value system
- Bridging religions through spirituality
- Inclusive development

The atmosphere in the school and the teacher's way of teaching, both inside and outside the class should inspire the youth.

Today, the students should make a promise to me. The promise has many parts, and I know you will fulfil them all.

1. I will have a goal and work hard to achieve that goal. I realize that aiming small is a crime.
2. I will work with integrity and succeed with integrity.
3. I will be a good member of my family, a good member of the society, a good member of the nation and a good member of the world.
4. I will always try to save or better someone's life, without any discrimination of caste, creed, language, religion or community.
5. I will always protect and enhance the dignity of every human life without any bias.
6. I will always remember the importance of time. My motto will be 'Let not my winged days, be spent in vain'.
7. I will always work for clean planet Earth and clean energy.
8. My national flag flies in my heart and I will bring glory to my nation.

(*from* Address and interaction with the students of Bijnor, 21 July 2015)

Creating a Culture of Excellence

When you wish upon a star,
Makes no difference who you are
Anything your heart desires
Will come to you.

Let me begin by sharing an important experience which I had during my education at Madras Institute of Technology, Chennai.

While I was studying aeronautical engineering in MIT, Chennai (1954-57), during the third year of my course, I was assigned a project to design a low-level attack aircraft together with six other colleagues. I was given the responsibility of system design and system integration. Also, I was responsible for the aerodynamic and structural design of the project. The other five members of my team took up the design of propulsion, control, guidance, avionics and instrumentation systems of the aircraft. My design teacher Professor Srinivasan, who was then the director of MIT, was our guide.

After we had worked on the project for some time, he reviewed the project and declared my work to be gloomy and disappointing. He refused to lend an ear to my difficulties in bringing together a database from multiple designers. I asked for a month's time to complete the task, since I had to get the inputs from five of my colleagues without which I could not complete the system design. Professor Srinivasan told me, 'Look, young man, today is Friday afternoon. I give you three days' time. If by Monday morning I don't get the configuration design, your scholarship will be stopped.' This gave me a big jolt. The scholarship was my lifeline. If it was stopped I would not be able to continue with my studies. There was no other way out but to complete the task of design. My team and I realised we needed to work together round the clock. We didn't sleep that night and worked at the drawing board skipping our dinner. On Saturday, I took just an hour's break. On Sunday morning, I was near completion, when I felt someone's presence in my laboratory. It was Professor Srinivasan studying my progress. After looking at my work, he patted and hugged me affectionately. He had these words of appreciation: 'I knew I was putting you under stress and asking you to meet a difficult deadline. You have done a great job in system design.'

One of the important lessons I learnt from my engineering education was the importance of system development, system integration and system management. This integrated learning experience assisted me in various phases of my career.

The way in which Professor Srinivasan reviewed the work, it really injected an understanding of the value of time by each team member and brought out the best from the team. I realized that if something important is at stake, the human mind gets ignited and the working capacity gets enhanced manifold. That's exactly what happened. This is one of the techniques of building talent.

The message here is that the young in the organization, whatever be their specialization, should be trained to understand multiple disciplines and projects, which will prepare them for new products, innovation and undertaking higher organizational responsibilities. A teacher has to be a coach like Professor Srinivasan.

In January 2006, the New Horizons rocket clocked the fastest launch ever recorded when it blasted off at excess of 36,000 miles per hour, crossing the moon in just nine hours. Capping a journey of 3 billion miles, the spacecraft took just three minutes to cross the diameter of Pluto. While most spacecraft depend on solar energy to power their on-board systems, this one was powered by nuclear fuel— aptly, plutonium—that gives off heat as it decays. The fuel is designed to last until the late 2020s or even beyond. The project chiefs had estimated there was a 1-in-10,000 chance that a debris strike could destroy New Horizons as it soared just 7,750 miles (12,472 km). It will take about sixteen months for New Horizons to transmit back all the thousands of images and measurements taken during its pass by Pluto to Earth but by that time, the spacecraft would have travelled even deeper into the Kuiper Belt, heading for a possible follow-on mission beyond the dwarf planet Pluto.

I mention this episode to make you understand the possibilities that exist for you to change the old ways of thinking and achieving something new and exciting. I was reading a book, *Empires of the Mind* by Denis Waitley. This book talks about what type of world are we facing now. What was there yesterday and what is there today? After reading it, I have modified certain points of the author. I have also added a third line which relates to leadership. The book says, 'What worked yesterday, won't work today.'

1. Yesterday: natural resources defined power
    Today: knowledge is power

Institutions should empower themselves with knowledge

2. Yesterday: hierarchy was the model
    Today: synergy is the mandate
    Institutions that enable the intersection of multiple faculties will achieve their mission goals

3. Yesterday: leaders commanded and controlled
    Today: leaders empower and coach
    Institutions should be sensitive to the needs of sustainable development

4. Yesterday: shareholders came first
    Today: customers come first
    Institutions should inculcate sensitivity towards the needs of all stakeholders

5. Yesterday: employees took orders
    Today: teams make decisions
    Institutions need to promote team spirit

6. Yesterday: seniority signified status
    Today: creativity drives status
    Institutions will be judged by how they promote innovation and creativity

7. Yesterday: production determined availability
    Today: competitiveness is the key
    Institutions will constantly evolve and become more competitive with knowledge, management and technology

8. Yesterday: value was an extra
    Today: value is everything
    Institutions need to inculcate value addition at every level

9. Yesterday: everyone was a competitor
   Today: everyone is a customer
   Institutions must value feedback and take action based on that
10. Yesterday: profits were earned through expediency
    Today: work with integrity and succeed with integrity
    Institutions have to imbibe the concept of working with integrity and succeeding with integrity, and act as promoters of such a culture among their students

The culture of excellence is driven by innovation and creativity. A nation's economic development is powered by competitiveness. Competitiveness is powered by knowledge. Knowledge is powered by technology. Technology is powered by innovation. Technology and innovation are powered by resource investment. Innovation opens up new vistas of knowledge and new dimensions to our imagination to make everyday life more meaningful and richer in depth and content. Innovation is born out of creativity.

In a knowledge society, we have to innovate continuously. Innovations come through creativity. Creativity comes from beautiful minds. It can be anywhere and in any part of the world. It may start from a fisherman's hamlet, or a farmer's household, or a dairy farm, or cattle breeding centre, or it could emanate from classrooms, or labs or industries, or R&D centres. Creativity has multi-dimensions like inventions, discoveries and innovations. A creative mind has the ability to imagine or invent something new by combining, changing or reapplying existing ideas. A creative person has to have the attitude to accept change and newness, a willingness to play with ideas and possibilities, a flexibility of outlook and the habit of enjoying what is good all the while looking for ways to improve it. Creativity is a process through which we can continuously improve ideas and find unique solutions by making gradual alterations and refinements to our works. The important aspect of creativity is seeing the same thing as everybody else, but thinking of something different. Innovation and creativity ultimately results into the culture of excellence.

Excellence in thinking and action is the foundation for any mission. What is excellence? Friends, you all belong to the youth community, which should be filled with a culture of excellence. Excellence does not come by accident. It is a process, where an individual or organization or nation continuously strives to better oneself. The performance standards are set by themselves, they work on their dreams with focus and are prepared to take calculated risks and do not be deterred by failures as they move towards their dreams. Then they step up their dreams, as they tend to reach the original targets. They strive to work to their potential, in the process, they increase their performance thereby multiplying further their potential, and this is an unending cycle. They are not in competition with anyone else, but themselves. That is the culture of excellence. I am sure each one of you will aspire to master this culture of excellence.

In the context of excellence, let me share with you how a street boy became a Nobel laureate.

Mario Capecchi had a difficult and challenging childhood. For nearly four years, Capecchi lived with his mother in a chalet in the Italian Alps. When World War II broke out, his mother, along with other Bohemians, was sent to the concentration camp at Dachau as a political prisoner. Anticipating her arrest by the Gestapo, she had sold all her possessions and given the money to some friends to help raise her son in their farm. Her son went to the farm where he had to grow wheat, harvest it and take it to the miller to be ground. But then the money which his mother left for him ran out and at the age of four and half years, he started living on the streets, sometimes joining gangs of other homeless children, sometimes living in orphanages and most of the time hungry. He spent a year in the city of Reggio Emelia, hospitalized for malnutrition where his mother found him on his ninth birthday after a year of searching. Within weeks, Capecchi and his mother sailed to America to join his uncle and aunt.

He started his third grade schooling afresh over there. He was interested in sports and went on to study political science. But he didn't find it interesting and changed to science, becoming a mathematics graduate in 1961 with a double major in Physics and Chemistry. Although he really liked Physics for its elegance and simplicity, he switched to molecular biology in graduate school on the advice of James D. Watson, who advised him that he should not be bothered about small things, since such pursuits are likely to produce only small answers.

Capecchi's objective was to do gene targeting. The experiments started in 1980 and by 1984, Capecchi had clear success. Three years later, he applied the technology to mice. In 1989, he developed the first mice with targeted mutations.

The technology created by Capecchi allows researchers to create specific gene mutations anywhere they choose in the genetic code of a mouse. By manipulating gene sequences in this way, researchers are able to mimic human disease conditions on animal subjects. What the research of Mario Capecchi means for human health is nothing short of amazing, his work with mice could lead to cures for Alzheimer's disease or even cancer. The innovations in genetics that Mario Capecchi achieved, won him the Nobel Prize in 2007.

Nobel laureate Capecchi life indeed reveals that

> When you wish upon a star,
> Makes no difference who you are,
> Anything your heart desires,
> Will come to you.

It is important to remember that science thrives when it converges to solve pressing challenges of the world and this is the 21st century requirement from engineers.

Sometime back, I was at the Harvard University where I visited laboratories of many eminent professors from the Harvard School of Engineering and Applied Sciences. I recall, how Professor Hongkun Park, showed me his invention of nano needles, which can pierce and deliver content into individual targeted cells. That's how nano particle sciences are shaping the bio sciences. On the other hand, Professor Vinod Manoharan showed how bio sciences are shaping nano material science as well. He is using DNA material to design self-assembling particles. When a particular type of DNA is applied on a particle at the atomic level, he is able to generate a prefixed behaviour and automatic assembly from them. This could be our answer to self-assembly of devices and colonies in deep space without human intervention as envisioned by Dr K. Erik Drexler. Thus, within a single research building, I saw how two different sciences are shaping each other without any iron curtain between the technologists. This way in which the sciences will shape each other and our future is something students of today need to understand and be ready for it.

Similarly, when I visited the University of Edinburgh, United Kingdom, I met Professor Siddharthan Chandran who showed me the Anne Rowling Regenerative Neurology Clinic. I was particularly impressed by the work being conducted in the field of early detection of mental and neural disorders. Professor Chandran showed his work on deploying technologies typically used by eye care professionals, and using that to help detect neural disorders. Using optical scanner devices, his team was mapping the inside of the eye, particularly the retina. They are going further and targeting the optical nerve, a small opening into the retina which carries neurons and photo receptors from the eye to the brain. Using advanced technologies they are able to 'peep' down the optical nerves by millimetres and make a longitudinal and cross-section image of it.

I read an article in the journal *Science* which talked about the latest DNA nano devices created at the Technische Universitaet Muenchen (TUM), including a robot with movable arms, a book that opens and closes, a switchable gear, and an actuator. But there is something special about this project. It demonstrates a

19

breakthrough in the science of using DNA as a programmable building material for nano-meter-scale structures and machines. Results reveal a new approach to joining—and reconfiguring—modular 3D building units, by fitting together complementary shapes, like puzzle pieces, instead of zipping together strings of base pairs. This not only opens the way for practical nano-machines with moving parts, but also offers a toolkit that makes it easier to program their self-assembly. This is a new field popularly known as 'DNA origami' in reference to the traditional Japanese art of paper folding. The program is advancing quickly towards practical applications. The researchers can control the joining of the nano-particles by altering the chemical ion concentration of the individual pieces. They are also controlling the joining pattern using temperature controls. Such controlled assembly robots can be useful for deep space applications or for fighting germs and pathogens inside the human body. Thus, by using the bioscience of DNA interaction, with physics of temperature, chemistry of ion concentration they are realizing the mechanics of robotic assembly which can be potentially useful in space science or the medical field.

Globally, a new aspect is being introduced, which is that of ecology. The demand is shifting towards development of sustainable systems which are technologically superior. This is the new dimension of the 21st century knowledge society, where science and environment will go together. Thus the new age model would be four dimensional and bio-nano-info-eco based. When technologies and systems converge, obviously one important aspect is 'systems thinking and implementation'.

While, successful scientists surely make a lot of wealth, but their motivation is always beyond money. They think in terms of what change they can bring about in other peoples' life. Science is driven by compassion and empathy often to alleviate the pains of humanity.

Look at the telephone; it would remind you of a unique scientist, Alexander Graham Bell. He, besides being a great inventor, was also a man of great compassion and service. In fact, much of the research which led to the development of the telephone was directed at finding solutions to the challenges of hearing impaired people and helping them to be able to listen and communicate. Bell's mother and wife were both hearing impaired and it profoundly changed Bell's outlook to science. He aimed to make devices which would help the hearing impaired. He started a special school in Boston to teach hearing impaired people in novel ways. It was these lessons which inspired him to work with sound and led to the invention of the telephone. Can you guess the name of the most famous student of Alexander Graham Bell? It was Helen Keller, the great author, activist and poet who was hearing and visually impaired. About her teacher, she once said that Bell dedicated his life to the penetration of that 'inhuman silence which separates and estranges'.

Finally I would like to ask you, what would you like to be remembered for? You have to evolve yourself and shape your life. Write your dreams down on a piece of paper. That page may be a very important page in the book of human history. You will be remembered for creating that one page in the history of the nation—whether that page is the page of invention, the page of innovation, or the page of discovery, or the page of creating societal change, or a page of removing poverty or the page of finding new technologies for humankind.

(from Address and interaction at
R.V. Institute of Technology, Bijnor, 21 July 2015)

Ignited Minds of the Youth

The power of the youth will definitely make a change.

Today, I would like to share how the ignited minds of the youth can lead to great and purposeful life so that societies will prosper and thereby, the nation and the world. This talk is about 'Ignited minds of the youth and the great challenges'.

Let me share with you a beautiful experience when I visited Greece in April 2007. I was negotiating and climbing towards the mountain top of Acropolis in Athens. On the way, I came across a group of 150 Greek students. They were friendly and the teachers accompanying them came forward and introduced the students. They said, they were very happy to see the Indian president and that the children would like to hear from him a few words. On my mind at that moment was the great personalities the land of Greece had given to the world: Socrates, Plato and Aristotle. The words of Plato were ringing in my mind when I saw the young students. He said: 'Our aim in founding the State was not the disproportionate happiness of any one class, but the greatest happiness of the whole.' This was said 2,400 years ago.

Similarly, around the same period Tamil poet Saint Thiruvalluvar said, 'The important elements that constitute a nation are: being disease free; high earning capacity; high productivity; harmonious living and strong defence'. How can all these elements be provided to citizens of every nation?

With these thoughts, I made up my mind about what to say to the students and the youth of Greece. I slowly repeated line by line, a hymn, which I normally hear in Indian spiritual centres.

Righteousness

Where there is righteousness in the heart,
There is beauty in the character.
When there is beauty in the character,
there is harmony in the home.
When there is harmony in the home,
There is an order in the nation.
When there is order in the nation,
There is peace in the world.

Not only the students repeated the words with me but also the tourists who were around the Acropolis at the time repeated and there was all-round ovation. I realized how people from multiple nations, both young and experienced were inspired by the thought of righteousness in the heart irrespective of their nationality. Righteousness in the heart is the starting point for creating great individuals, families, nations and ultimately a great Earth.

The ignited minds of the youth is the most powerful resource on the Earth. I am convinced that the power of the youth, if properly directed, will bring about transformed humanity by meeting its challenges and bring peace and prosperity.

Let us now consider two major problems the world faces: one is, out of 7 billion people, majority of the population in certain continents live below the poverty line, 50 per cent of the population do not have access to safe drinking water, and many do not have access to quality education. What can the youth of the world contribute to make this situation better? If every educated person spreads literacy to at least five others in their life then we can make a beginning in eradicating illiteracy? Can the youth spread the message of water conservation? Can the youth come with 'out-of-box solutions' for solving water scarcity?

I have proposed a movement called Lead India 2020 which is a youth movement, with the mission for young students based on the ten-point oath which I have specially designed.

The oath given to the youth says that they can make a difference to society in the areas of literacy, environment, social justice, minimizing the rural urban divide and aim for national development even as they work hard for an individual goal. I insist that small aim is a crime. The development of youth has multiple dimensions. The youth must work hard improving their knowledge with a career goal and also serve the family, society, the nation to which he or she belongs to and humanity as a whole. All are complementary to each other.

While talking about good deeds, I am reminded of the advice given to Mahatma Gandhi by his mother. She said, 'Son, in your entire lifetime, if you can save or better someone's life, your birth as a human being and your life is a success.'

This advice made a deep impact on Gandhiji's mind and he worked for humanity throughout his life.

Let me narrate another instance of selflessness.

During the year 2003, when I was visiting the state of

Arunachal Pradesh, I also visited a Buddhist monastery at Tawang, situated at an altitude of 3,500 metre. I was in the monastery for almost a full day. I observed that in all the nearby villages, the young and old were radiating an inner happiness in spite of severe winter conditions. At the 400-year-old Tawang monastery, I saw monks of all age groups in a state of serenity. I was asking myself what is the unique feature of Tawang and its surrounding villages which makes people and monks to be at peace with themselves. I asked the chief monk about this. He smiled and said, 'You are the President of India. You will know all about us and the whole nation.' Again, I said, 'It is very important for me, please give me your thoughtful analysis.'

There was a beautiful golden image of Lord Buddha. The Chief Monk assembled nearly 100 monks of various ages. We sat amidst them. There he gave a short discourse, which I would like to share with you. He said, 'In the world today, we have a problem of distrust and unhappiness that transforms into violence. But in this monastery we believe that when you remove "I" and "me" from the mind, you will eliminate ego; if you get rid of the ego, hatred towards fellow human beings will vanish; if the hatred goes out of the mind, the violence in thinking and action will disappear; if violence in our mind is taken away, peace springs in human minds.'

I realized the meaning of this beautiful equation for a peaceful life. But the difficult part for the individual is how to remove the ethos of 'I' and 'me'. For this, we need education and values to be inculcated from a young age.

In my search for evolving a peaceful and prosperous society,

I got another answer elsewhere. I visited an ancient Christian monastery in Bulgaria, where I had a discussion with highly experienced monks. I told them about the lesson from Tawang. The monks there agreed, and also added that forgiveness is the foundation of a good life.

Similarly, I had a memorable experience in the birth place of Swami Vivekananda, a young monk of India who could keep the audience spell bound in eastern and western society with his inspirational messages of spirituality and practical aspects of life. I explained the Tawang experience to the disciples and they agreed that it was beautiful. They added that developing a habit of always giving will add to peace and happiness.

When I visited Ajmer Sharif I participated in the Friday namaz. Here, the Sufi expert told me that Almighty's creation, man, has been challenged with another powerful creation of Shaitan. Only good deeds lead to good thinking, good thinking results in actions radiating love as commanded by the Almighty.

The message from all these and other spiritual thinkers is that there are many ideas and spiritual thoughts which transcend religions, geographies and time. If only we could bridge the spirituality among religions and nations, many of the problems like the gaps between haves and have nots, deprivation causing unrest leading to extremism, the remnants of past animosities and war and several other road blocks to peace and prosperity can be tackled. I am sure the global youth will work on this theme for a safe world.

On 28 September 2011, I addressed a combined group of students from Harvard University and MIT on the topic

'Leadership, Youth and Global Engagement'. Over 500 students hailing from USA and many different continents participated in my lecture. After the lecture, the students formed nine groups and prepared nine sets of questions. Of the nine sets, three questions came from USA team, two questions from the Asian team, and a few general questions. The USA team asked me, why do you make missiles and atom bombs in India, when your nation needs the basic facilities like education and healthcare for all your citizens? My answer to the question was, if you study Indian history of 5,000 years, it can be seen that only for 600 years India was ruled by Indians. In the remaining period, we were invaded and ruled by many kingdoms hailing from different countries. The last of such rulers were the British who ruled India for over 300 years. We achieved our independence after ninety years of struggle. So, history had taught us that we must have minimum strength of adequately equipped Armed Forces so that India can preserve its hard earned freedom and work towards prosperity and peace. When we are surrounded by many nuclear weapon states, we have no other option but to maintain a minimum force. This doctrine is applicable for all the nations with similar geopolitical situation. However, we have a doctrine of 'no first use'. Of course, India spends less than 3 per cent of GDP on defence. India must preserve its hard-earned sovereignty and work in an atmosphere of strength as is true for many other countries in this region.

The next question came from the Asian team that was presided over by a student from Pakistan. She asked me, 'Dr Kalam can you tell me, at any time in present or future, can

India and Pakistan work together for the prosperity and peace of their citizens?' To this question I replied, 'After all we both are of the same form. We have seen European nations fighting among themselves for hundreds of years and they lead the world into two World Wars. But today, the 27 nations of Europe have formed a European Union and have a Parliament of 800 members with a mission of promoting prosperity and peace in the continent. I am sure, history will one day repeat in Asia and in another few decades' time, it is possible India and Pakistan may work together for prosperity and peace of both the nations. Even the SAARC nations may transform into a dynamic region like EU in South-Asia.

The third question came from a MIT student. 'Dr Kalam, please tell me, in the next twenty years, what type of technological changes do you expect to take place?' I acknowledged that it is a very good question. I said, my visualization of futuristic technology upto the year 2030 is a convergence of sciences and technologies. That means, bio-science, nano-science, information-science and environmental science will converge, reciprocate and create new technologies for the betterment of the society.

There will be, in the near future, more than ever the need for compassionate leadership. Let me share with you now about a book called *Everyday Greatness*. Here's an experience which happened in Mexico. A riot was raging in La Mesa Prison in Mexico. Twenty-five hundred prisoners were packed into a compound, which had been built for only 600. They angrily hurled broken bottles at the police who fired back with machine guns. Then came a startling sight. A tiny five feet two inches,

31

sixty-three-year-old woman calmly got into the crowd, with outstretched hands, in a simple gesture of peace. Ignoring the shower of bullets, she stood quietly and asked everyone to stop. Incredibly everyone did. No one else in the world, but Sister Antonia could have done this. Why did the people listen to her? All because of her decades of service to the prisoners. She had sacrificed all her life for the sake of the prisoners who lived in the midst of murderers, thieves and drug lords all of whom she called her sons. She attended to their needs round the clock, procured antibiotics, distributed eyeglasses, washed bodies for the burial and counselled the suicidal. This selfless act of love and compassion generated a respect among the prisoners and that is why she could control them and urged them to do what she wanted them to do. What a great message for humanity! There's a leader with compassion for even prisoners, but we also need similar leaders with compassion for the voiceless millions in the world.

I'd like to share this event that I witnessed when I was a young boy of about ten years. In our house, periodically I used to see three different unique personalities meet. Pakshi Lakshmana Shastrigal, who was the head priest of the famous Rameshwaram temple and a Vedic scholar, Rev Father Bodal, who built the first church in Rameswaram island and my father who was an imam in the mosque. All three of them used to sit and discuss the island's problems and find solutions. In addition, they initiated dialogues between communities with compassion. These connectivities quietly spread in the island like the fragrance from the flowers. The memory of the three men meeting always comes to my mind whenever I discuss the importance of dialogue between religions. India has had this advantage of integration of minds for thousands of years. Throughout the world, the need to have a frank dialogue among cultures, religions and civilizations is being felt now more than ever.

There are some events that bring together the whole world. We have seen how the launching of Sputnik by the Russians or Neil Armstrong's stepping on the moon electrified the entire youth of the world. When an Indian origin astronaut along with her colleagues was returning to Earth after a major space mission, the entire world prayed for their safe return. Cricket is followed avidly in the commonwealth while soccer has an European inspiration, and they represent intense competition and admiration across borders. Similarly, I have seen many instances of how art and music integrate the minds of the youth.

A few years back, when I met Mr Vladimir Putin, the President of Russia, we agreed on building a youth satellite where the youth from different countries can work together. Such working together will increase understanding, make them explore new avenues and the spirit of cooperation among the youth globally will prevail. The idea of a youth satellite as a joint venture of countries was born. I am glad, the space agencies of India and Russia put in efforts and the first youth satellite was launched on 20 April 2011 from Sriharikota, in the state of Andhra Pradesh. I had then suggested to the ISRO team to continue the series of youth satellites, so that you may also use this as a platform for developing collaborative projects, needed for scientific and technological developments and its applications and above all, it will lead to integration of minds.

Dear friends, if you ask me, how my life has been enriched for the last eighty-three years, I have to convey to all of you one message. The message is like this. When I reached the age of seventeen, I had one great companion. That companion was nothing but great books. Throughout my life, books enriched me. I would suggest and recommend all of you to read the following books:

- *Light from Many Lamps* by Lillian Eichler
- *Empires of the Mind* by Denis Waitley
- *Thirukkural* by Thiruvalluvar
- *Everyday Greatness* by Steven R. Covey
- *The Story of My Experiments with Truth* by Mahatma Gandhi

Earth is facing many conflicts both natural and man-made. As a youth, all of you have a responsibility to work for universal harmony by ironing out all the causes of conflicts. Are you ready to do so?

One of the important areas of work is moving towards clean green energy and a clean planet Earth. That means it is centred around on a mission for providing a good life to 7 billion people. If all of you work for this singular mission, then Earth will be free from fossil fuel. We will move away from costly fuel which is detrimental to the environment and achieve clean energy using solar power, nuclear power and bio-fuel. Certainly this mission challenge the innovative ability of the youth. I am confident the youth leaders will take up this challenge. The action starts from today onwards. Will you take up the challenge with an indomitable spirit?

Yes dear friends, the power of the youth will definitely make a change—a change that will bring prosperity of the nation and the world.

(*from* Address to students at BMICH, Colombo, 26 June 2015)

The Life-long Quest for Knowledge

Teachers can influence students not only by teaching but by also giving practical lessons in human values, particularly by their selfless giving of knowledge.

Dear friends, I would like to share with you a great event that happened on 18 Dec 2014. Indian Space Research Organisation's (ISRO) GSLV Mark III achieved its test mission successfully by travelling on an expected path on time. This proclaimed to the world that India will soon realize its dream of sending its astronauts into space. This was an experimental launch and the full-fledged launch is likely to take place in two years' time. The main purpose of this mission was to test the atmospheric characteristics and stability of the rocket. The 630-tonne rocket has gone up to 126 km and then the 4-tonne crew capsule which has enough space to accommodate three people detached and landed into the Bay of Bengal, 600 km from Port Blair and 1,600 km from the space station twenty minutes of blast off. Three parachutes controlled the crew module as per expected lines.

The system worked to the scheduled times perfectly. After launch, the heat shield separated, the Crew Module Atmospheric Re-entry Experiment (CARE) module separated from the launch vehicle, then the module worked in active control, aerodynamic deceleration phase started on expected lines, deceleration system initiation started at the right time and the apex cover separated exactly on time, the pilot chute ejection was initiated and drogue chute deployment started, the penultimate action of main parachute deployment was activated, and finally CARE module impacted on the Andaman sea within twenty minutes of the entire life-cycle.

GSLV Mark III has made ISRO self-reliant to launch big satellite for important societal applications such as solar power satellite and manned missions later. Some of you may one day become astronauts for ISRO's moon mission or Mars mission. My friends in ISRO say, the reason for the success of this mission is the creative and scientific minds of the youth who participated in this programme. I thought of sharing this information as I am certain it will inspire the youth to take up the pursuit of science.

The desire to study science or any other subject may come from people you meet as young people.

When I think of my childhood days, I am reminded of Shri Sivasubramania Iyer who taught me when I was studying in the fifth grade at the age of ten. Whenever my teacher entered into the classroom, we all saw in him a teacher radiating knowledge. He was a great teacher in our school. All of us loved to attend his class and hear him. One day, he was teaching about the flight of bird. He drew a diagram of a bird on the blackboard depicting the wings, tail and the body structure with the head. He explained how birds lift and fly. He also explained to us how they change direction while flying. For nearly twenty-five minutes he gave the lecture with lots of information on lift, drag, how the birds fly in a formation. At the end of the class, he wanted to know whether we had understood how the birds fly. I said I did not understand. When I said this, the teacher asked the other students whether they understood or not. Many students said that they also did not understand. Our response did not upset him, since he was a committed teacher.

Shri Iyer said that he would take all of us to the seashore. That evening the whole class was at the seashore of Rameswaram. We enjoyed the roaring sea waves knocking at the sandy hills in the pleasant evening. Birds were flying with sweet chirping voice. He showed the sea birds in formations of ten to twenty. We saw the marvellous formations of birds and were amazed. He showed us the birds and asked us to see that when the birds fly, what they looked like. We saw the wings flapping. He asked us to look at the tail portion alongwith flapping wings and twisting tail. We noticed closely and found that the birds in that condition flew in the direction they desired. Then he asked us a question, where is the bird's engine and how is it powered. He went on to explain that the bird is powered by its own life and the motivation of what it wants. All these things were explained to us within fifteen minutes. We all understood the whole dynamics from this practical example. Your teacher was a great teacher; he could give us a theoretical lesson coupled with a live practical example available from nature. This is real teaching.

For me, it was not merely an understanding of how a bird flies. From that evening, I thought that my future study had to be with reference to flight and flight systems. I am saying this because my teacher's teaching and the event that I witnessed decided my future career. Then one evening after the classes, I asked my teacher, 'Sir, please tell me, how to progress further in learning all about flight.' He patiently explained to me that I should complete my eighth class, go to high school, to engineering college that may lead to learning about flight. If I completed all my education with excellence, I might be able to do something connected with flight sciences. This advice and the bird flying lesson given by my teacher, really gave me a goal and a mission for my life. When I went to college, I took Physics. When I went to study engineering in Madras Institute of Technology, I took Aeronautical Engineering.

Thus my life was transformed to a rocket engineer, aerospace engineer and technologist. That one incident of my teacher teaching the lesson showing the live example proved to be a turning point in my life which eventually shaped my profession and enabled me to fly.

Another great teacher, who is a living legend now, is Professor Chinnadurai. He taught me Physics, particularly Nuclear Physics. The way the professor taught, many students started loving the subject. When he was taking lessons, he used to give reference articles and good reference books that the students could refer to and read. He ensured that we all referred to good Physics textbooks during the lecture instead of only reading the notes. This widened the horizon of the learning. Professor Chinnadurai still lives in Dindugal and I meet him and pay my respects whenever I am in that area. The method of his teaching was important in making the student a lifelong independent learner, which is essential for the continuous growth of an individual, and thereby the nation. The best learning takes place when the teacher infuses a creative learning habit in the students and makes it an enjoyable part of life-long quest for knowledge. Even today, whenever I meet him, he radiates a sense of enlightenment.

These examples show how teachers can influence the students not only by teaching but also giving practical lessons in human values, particularly the trait of selfless giving of knowledge. I am grateful to my college for helping me acquire knowledge and value systems in life.

Do you know about a man of science and about a life completely dedicated to innovation, creativity and scientific research? His most famous success was the astrophysical Chandrasekhar limit. The Chandra limit describes the maximum mass (greater than 1.44 solar mass) of a white dwarf star, or equivalently, the minimum mass for which a star will ultimately collapse into a neutron star or black hole following a supernova. The limit was first calculated by a scientist while on a ship from India to Cambridge, England. Yes, I am referring to Subramanyan Chandrasekhar, who lived his entire life for research on the cosmos.

There was a great woman scientist who is known for discovering radium. She won not one, but two Nobel Prizes, one for Physics and another for Chemistry. Who is she? She was Madam Curie. She discovered radium and was doing research on the effect of radiation on the human system. The same radiation which she discovered, affected her and she sacrificed her life for removing the pain in human life.

Now, to all the students gathered here, I would like to talk about the importance of creating a beautiful home environment.

A beautiful home—and we have 200 million homes in India—emanates from four dimensions. One comes from spiritual home, second comes from mother's happiness, third comes from transparency of the home and the fourth comes from providing a clean and green environment. This combination of four traits indeed brings about a happy home. Let us study, how we can achieve that.

Spiritual Home

Let us imagine a small family home with father, mother, a son and a daughter, or two sons or two daughters. In this home, both parents earn. I visualize in this little home, a little home library with at least ten great books and in this home parents inculcate the reading habit among their children by reading books during breakfast or during dinner. The whole family gets together for at least one meal so that they communicate and discuss freely. When they are all together on the dining table, the mother or the father takes a book from the home library narrates a story of ethics and moral values, and where the children participate in the discussion and offer their comments. Such a reading habit triggers the child to read the book in detail and collect more information on such stories. They put the lessons they learn thus in practice in their day-to-day life. Some children may also go to the school and discuss such instances with other children and so a larger community is benefitted. This is how the seeding of reading habits can be inculcated among the young minds. In addition, I visualize a little prayer room where every morning or night the whole family, including children prays and offers their thanks to the Almighty for receiving blessings.

This family time will become the time when knowledge and value systems are inculcated in children. Such children will carry out their responsibilities with a spirit of excellence, dedication and self esteem.

Making Mother Smile Mission

I am going to give you a mission that will lead to a happy home. Will you friends promise me that you will follow the suggestion that I am giving.

From today onwards, I will make my mother happy,
If my mother is happy, my home is happy,
If my home is happy, the society will be happy,
If societies are happy, the state will be happy,
If state is happy, the nation will be happy.

How many of you are willing to do the great mission of making your mothers happy?

A Transparent Home

As I said, we belong to a society of 200 million families. The first step towards creating a transparent society comes from a transparent home. There is a crying need in the nation to develop a transparent society, a corruption free society. Dear young members, I have a mission for the youth of the nation, that is the daughter or son of the family. Every one of you will know that corruption emanates from a few homes. It is estimated that 30 per cent of our Indian homes are corrupt. That means approximately 60 million houses may not be transparent. In such a situation, children should appreciate their father if he is fully transparent. At the same time, if he is not, children should use their love and affection and have the courage to say no to such practices. My conscience says, compared to any law against corruption, definitely this movement of the youth against corruption will be extremely effective. How many of you young friends will offer yourself to be a participant of such a great mission of making the home transparent?

Green Home Mission

Today there is climate change occurring on Earth. Deforestation, industrialization and transportation emitted carbon-dioxide, which has caused holes in the ozone layer leading to increased heating of the planet. This is the major cause of flood and drought. If the youth of the nation decide, they can definitely change the situation. Every Indian must take an oath that he or she will plant and nurture at least one tree. One fully grown tree absorbs 20 kg of carbon dioxide and emits 14 kg of oxygen. During our lifetime, if we plant ten trees and nurture them, we will have over ten billion trees. These ten billion trees can definitely help contain the climate change problem. Hence, I would suggest, each one of you to plant a tree and keep your home and the neighbourhood clean. Green home means not only the planting of trees but keeping the house and environment clean. You should not dump any garbage on the streets. You should take an oath that, you will not only keep the home clean, but also ensure that the street is clean.

All around us we see examples of great people who have served in industry, government, armed forces and arts and literature. When you are inspired by such well-known personalities, I would like to ask , what would you like to be remembered for? You have to evolve and shape your life.

(*from* Address and interaction with the students of Baldwin Institutions, Bangalore, 12 June 2015)

Managing the Journey of Life

These are the best days of your lives, when you are learning to grow wings and learning to fly.

Friends, one of the biggest challenges for the scientific and technology community for decades is earthquake prediction. Intensive research worldwide is essential in the area of earthquake prediction. I have seen a model in Iceland—a validated progress within the small area about 1,000 sq km. This was possible by following a database. Studies showed how the tremor in the form of a vibration builds up gradually and stress builds up few days and few hours before an earthquake. This model of earthquake validated nearly three decades database. What is needed for India is the following: we have to form an integrated team of geologists, material scientists, physicists, and remote sensing satellite experts, rock formation experts and oil exploration experts. Ideally, it should be a young team of members below the age of forty. The mission to be given to this team would be to predict an earthquake that will occur in the next twenty-four hours. This window of prediction should slowly be increased to before two days before seven days before four weeks with certain probability. This may be a mission of ten years for young people. Research on forecasting will bring great name and India will be protected from the devastations of earthquakes. This challenge of earthquake prediction is put up on my blog www.3billion. org and has been receiving great responses.

Before you embark on a path of intense research you also

need to understand about 'Managing the Journey of Life'.

In this context, I will talk to you about four important aspects in life with my experiences—having an aim, acquiring knowledge, working hard towards your dream even in the times of difficulty and then finally, how to manage failures and success in life.

Behind every successful venture and every inspiring career you will find an unflinching aim which was often set early in life. Having an aim in life gives purpose to every action and orientation to every result.

Before you enter into your professional life, it is important to forge your unique aim in life which will steer your efforts towards a well-defined goal for the rest of your life. It will always remind you of your goals and give you strength.

Having an aim in life is incomplete until you are able to acquire the right knowledge needed to accomplish that aim. It is your duty to make the best use of the resources, people and networks made available to you by your parents and in your schools and colleges to acquire the optimal knowledge needed to propel you towards your goal. Knowledge will give you greatness, and will help you accomplish difficult missions.

I would like to share with all of you the story of my teacher Professor Satish Dhawan. I was working in Delhi at the Ministry of Defence. Later I joined the Defence Research and Development Organisation (DRDO) in 1958 at the Aeronautical Development Establishment, Bangalore. There, on the advice of the director, I took up the development of a hovercraft. Hovercraft design needed the development of a ducted contra-rotating propeller for creating a smooth flow balancing the torques. I did not know how to design a contra-rotating propeller though I knew how to design a conventional propeller. Some of my friends told me that I can approach Professor Satish Dhawan of the Indian Institute of Science, who was well known for his aeronautical research, for help in designing the ducted contra-rotating propeller.

I took permission from my director Dr Mediratta and went to Professor Dhawan who was sitting in a small room in the Indian Institute of Science with a lot of books all around him. There was also a blackboard on the wall. I explained the problem to him about my project work. He told me that it was really a challenging task and he would teach me the design if I attended his classes at the Indian Institute of Science between 2 p.m. and 3 p.m. on all Saturdays for the next six weeks. I started doing so. I found that he was a visionary teacher. He prepared the schedule for the entire course and wrote it on the black board so we could be prepared for all the new topics as he taught them. He also gave me the reference material and books I should read before I started attending the course. I considered this as a great opportunity and started meeting him regularly. Before commencing each class, he would ask critical questions and assess my understanding of the subject. That was the first time that I realized how a good teacher prepares himself for teaching with meticulous planning and prepares the student for the acquisition of knowledge. This process continued for the next six weeks. I understood the principles and finally got the capability for designing a ducted contra-rotating propeller.

Professor Dhawan told me that I was ready for developing the propeller for a hovercraft configuration. That was the time I realized that Professor Satish Dhawan was not only a teacher but also a fantastic development engineer of aeronautical systems.

Later during the critical phases of contra-rotating propeller system testing Professor Dhawan was with me and helped in finding solutions to the problems. After reaching the smooth test phase, the propeller went through 50 hours of continuous testing. Professor Satish Dhawan witnessed the test himself and congratulated me. That was a great day for me when I saw the propeller designed by my team performing to the mission requirement in the hovercraft. However, at that time, I did not realize that Professor Satish Dhawan would become Chairman, ISRO and that I would get the opportunity to work with him as a Project Director in the development of Satellite Launch Vehicle SLV-3 for injecting the Rohini satellite into the orbit.

That was the first design in my career. It gave me the confidence to deal with many complex aerospace systems in future. The hovercraft could fly just above the ground level carrying two passengers. I was the first pilot for this hovercraft and I could control and manoeuvre the vehicle in any direction. Above all, I learnt that in a project, problems would always crop up; we should not allow problems to be our masters but we should defeat the problems. Then success will sparkle.

In order to achieve great aims, one needs to work relentlessly towards the goal. Constant effort with application of proper knowledge can help overcome difficulties and scale steep heights.

I was fortunate to come under the mentorship of three gurus,

Professor Vikram Sarabhai, Dr Brahm Prakash and Professor Satish Dhawan. In 1973, I was entrusted with a major national project of developing the first Satellite Launch Vehicle SLV-3. I was able to achieve the project in seven years with a great team. None of us knew totally about SLV-3 or its subsystems. We learnt, dreamt, experimented, failed, recovered and succeeded. Everybody was innovative, everybody questioned everybody else. Each one enjoyed the success of others. My team members were all good, energetic and tough guys. I had a difficult but pleasant duty to manage these great guys. Even now I relish this experience. They all grew to take up major responsibilities in ISRO.

When you set upon difficult missions, it will bring difficult challenges which may sometimes produce temporary setbacks. The test of a human being is in accepting the failure and to keep trying until he or she succeeds. Managing failures is a quality which is the essence of leadership. Let me now tell you an experience in this regard from my professional life.

When I think of Professor Satish Dhawan, many incidents come to my mind. I would like to share with you again, one important incident, which is a valuable lesson to the younger generation. I was the project director of the first experimental launch of SLV-3. On 10 August 1979, the vehicle took off beautifully at T-0 and the first stage gave predicted performance. The second stage was initiated, but within a few seconds, we witnessed the vehicle in a tumbling motion and we lost the flight to the Bay of Bengal. It was 8 a.m. in the morning. The whole team in spite of working all day and night for several days, got busy in collecting the data and trying to establish the reason for the flight failure. Meanwhile, I was called by Professor Satish Dhawan to attend a press conference. Before the press conference, he told me that he was going to handle the situation and I should be present with many of the senior scientists and technologists. The press conference room was overflowing with media-persons. There was gloom, many questions were posed, some very powerful, thoughtful and also criticisms. There, Professor Satish Dhawan, announced, 'Friends, today we had the experimental launch of SLV-3 to put the Rohini satellite in the orbit. It was a partial success. It is our first mission of proving multiple technologies in a launch vehicle. We have proved many technologies in this launch but still we have to prove some more. We have tumbled but not fallen flat. Above all, I realize my team members have to be given all the technological support for the next mission to succeed.' Subsequently, a failure analysis board established the cause and we proceeded with the preparation for the second launch.

The second mission of SLV-3 took place on 18 July 1980. It was six-thirty in the morning. The whole nation's attention was trained on SHAR launch complex in Sriharikota, now named after Professor Satish Dhawan as a great tribute to him. The mission teams were busy during the countdown, carefully watching the flight sequence. At T-0 the vehicle took off and we witnessed a textbook trajectory. After nearly 600 seconds of the flight, I realized every stage had given the required velocity including the fourth stage. I made an announcement, 'Mission director calling all stations. The SLV-3 has given the required velocity and right altitude to put Rohini satellite in the orbit. Our down range stations and global stations will get the orbit of the satellite within an hour.' There was thunderous applause from all the stations and from the visitors' gallery.

The most important thing happened then. Professor Satish Dhawan asked me to handle the press conference with our team members.

There are two messages I would like to convey here. First is about the resilience and courage to pick ourselves up and work towards a resurgence after a setback. Second is about the role of a leader in managing failure. The leader should give the credit of the success to the team members. When failure comes the leaders should absorb the failures and protect the team members. I could not get this beautiful education of failure management in any of the textbooks or studied it at any of the institutes at that time.

Let me now give you a memorable event from my professional work in missile technology, which also gave me bliss. This was my experience creating FRO (Floor Reaction Orthosis) calliper for polio-affected children. During my visit to one of the hospitals in Hyderabad, I found many children were struggling to walk with an artificial limb weighing over 4 kg. At the request of Professor Prasad of NIMS, who was the head of the orthopaedic department at that time, I asked my AGNI missile friends why we cannot use the composite material used for AGNI heat shield for fabricating FROs for polio-affected patients. They immediately said it was possible. We worked on this project for some time and came up with a

FRO for the child weighing around 400 gm in place of 4 kg, that is, exactly, 1/10th of the weight which the children were carrying. The doctors helped us fit the new lightweight FRO on the children and they started walking and running around. Their parents were also present as their children were fitted with the new callipers. Tears rolled down on all of their faces at the joy of seeing their children running with the light callipers. With the lightweight device provided by the hospital they could run, ride a bicycle and do all sorts of things which they had been denied for a long time. The removal of the pain and the freedom attained by the children gave me a state of bliss which I never experienced during any other achievement in my life.

I believe each one of my young friends can and will work to be a part of the one million enlightened youth in the country and bring about societal transformation.

For this, wherever you are, the thought that will always come to your mind is what process or product can you innovate, invent or discover.

Always remember that these are the best days of your lives, when you are learning to grow wings and learning to fly. Don't let these precious days go in vain.

Whatever be the field you choose to specialise in, you have to think big, work hard and persevere to realize the goal.

Great scientific, technological and compassionate minds, good teachers, good books and good internal environment are required to bring about development.

Each of you must firmly believe that no problem can defeat you. You have to say: I will become the captain of the problem, defeat the problem and succeed.

We all need to work for removing the problems faced by the planet in the areas of water, energy, habitat, waste management and environment through the application of science and technology.

We need to realize that we are as young as our faith and as old as our doubts. We are also as young as our self-confidence and as old as our fears. We are as young as our hopes and as old as our despairs.

We will develop faith, self-confidence and hope.

(*from* Address and interaction with students at
Cochin College of Science and Technology,
Muvattupuzha, 6 May 2015)

Innovation and Creativity

In a knowledge society, we have to make innovations continuously. Innovations come through creativity. Creativity comes from beautiful minds.

When knowledge becomes an important part of the economy, then society focuses more on empowerment and all-round development rather than only on fulfilling basic needs. The education system is improved as there is interactivity and creativity in teaching and motivated self-learning. Both formal and informal education focus on values, merit and quality. After such an education, those who enter the work force will be knowledgeable, self-empowered and have the flexibility in their thinking and skill sets to deal with different issues and problems. The type of work they do may be less structured and require development of relevant software instead of being structured and hardware driven. Managers will emphasize more on delegating responsibilities rather than expecting employees to only take orders. Finally, the economy will mostly be driven by knowledge-driven industries.

I would like to share here a message with you. It is a message that connects mind, resource, personality, team and leader. Twenty-first century leaders need to have a new dimension with knowledge, most importantly the leader should work with integrity and succeed with integrity.

I have mentioned the idea of 'What worked yesterday, will not work today'. We need to constantly evaluate the changing realities of the world around us and innovate and adapt.

I have mentioned the following aspects of leadership:

- Leadership should empower itself with knowledge.
- Leadership will enable in the intersection of multiple faculties in order to achieve mission goals.
- Leadership will enrich itself through an understanding of the needs of sustainable development.
- Leadership should inculcate sensitivity to the needs of all the stakeholders.
- Leadership has to promote team spirit.
- Leadership will be judged by innovation and how it has promoted creativity.
- Leadership will constantly evolve and become more competitive with knowledge, management and technology.
- Leadership will inculcate value addition at every level.
- Leadership will value feedback and take action based on that.
- Leaders will work with integrity and succeed with integrity and act as promoters of such a culture in their subordinates.

I was studying the development patterns and the dynamics of connectivity between nations, especially in trade and business. As you all know the world has a few developed countries and many developing countries. What is the dynamics between them and what connects them? A developed country has to market its products in a competitive way to different countries to maintain its position as a developed country. The developing country also have to market their products to other countries in a competitive way if they want to become developed. Competitiveness is the common factor between the two types of countries. The more successful one is the one who achieves three dimensions: quality of the product, cost effectiveness and supply in time. This dynamics of competitiveness in marketing of products by developing and developed countries is called the law of development.

In this context, the time has come to launch new technology that will improve the connectivity in the remote areas of the nation. Today, we have 900 million mobile phone connections nationally. It is estimated that by the end of 2017, there will be over 500 million mobile-based Internet users in the nation from the current number of 160 million. Many of these new users will be in rural areas. Currently, a majority of 600,000 villages, where 70 per cent of the population lives are not connected with high speed Internet connectivity so far. Even 3G mobile network connections are not available in majority of the rural areas.

Here, I would like to share one information, that of a new type of fibre optic cable developed by researchers in US and Netherlands that has smashed data transfer records, managing to squeeze 255 terabits of information per second down a single strand of glass fibre.

Today, India is currently ranked 118th in the world in broadband speed with an average speed of 1.7 mbps compared to over 20 mbps in Japan and Hong Kong. Today, India has approximately 14 million km fibre laid over the last one decade connecting few cities and some districts and it is envisaged to reach 30 million km 2017, probably reaching up to district and block level. If we need to bridge the digital divide between the rural and urban areas, it is essential to connect 2.5 lakh panchayats and 600,000 villages with fibre optic cables. If we need to do that approximately we need 6 lakh cable km and 15 million fibre km to connect 2.5 lakh village panchayats. Now if we need to connect 600,000 villages and the cities, then we need to lay maximum of 400 million fibre km. The challenge of realizing 'Digital India' is to create 400 million fibre km infrastructure. It is reported that China is creating 200 million fibre km every year to bridge the digital divide. The most challenging component for us will be laying the fibre cable underground with an effective project management, process management to achieve the target on time.

Since the fibre optics cable technology can go with the high tension electrical wire, also the hybrid fibre, copper, aluminium cables can transmit power, data together without any electrical interference and loss, if we lay the optical fibre along with the existing electrical power lines, we can reach out to the entire country. Hence appropriate policy should be evolved to connect the optical fibre along with power lines.

Until and unless the villages are connected and have Wi-Fi access, the digital divide is bound to exist. Hence, I would urge all of you in engineering, technology and communication to work with the government, public and private institutions to evolve a road map to bring high speed Wi-Fi access to villages through the combination of fibre cable, Wi-Fi and 3G/4G connectivity. Once this is possible, we can provide to these new user segments a reliable services which is seamless, fast and free from breakdown and at the same time cost-effective.

I would like to touch upon another important area which will have a huge impact in human lives. This is Artificial Intelligence (AI). As you are aware, Artificial Intelligence can enhance human endeavour by complementing what people can do. Amalgamated teams of humans and algorithms will become the norm in all sorts of pursuits. Supported by AI, doctors will have augmented ability to spot cancers in medical images; speech-recognition algorithms running on smartphones will bring the Internet to rural populations; digital assistants will help in academic research; image classification algorithms will allow wearable computers to layer useful information onto people's views of the real world. (Source: *The Economist*, May 9-15, 2015).

I was studying the Global Competitiveness Report for the year 2014–15. There, I found that in terms of Global Competitive Index ranking, Switzerland is ranked 1, Singapore is ranked 2, US is ranked 3, UAE is 12, Korea is 26, China is 28 and India is 71. Our performance in a range of competitiveness index needs to be improved. Growth competitiveness is determined by the innovative ability of an organization. This innovation arises from initiatives taken by the institution and the R&D productivity of the firm, shaped by policies and nature of local institutions. We need to work to improve the competitiveness index and aim to reach the top 10 among the nations of the world in the next five years. This requires the combined efforts of researchers, technologists, production engineers, business leaders and above all support from the political system

Innovation opens up new vistas of knowledge and new dimensions to our imagination to make everyday life more meaningful and richer in depth and content. Innovation is born out of creativity.

In a knowledge-based society, we have to make innovations continuously. Innovations come through creativity. Creativity comes from beautiful minds. It can be anywhere and from any part of the world.

I am sure there will always be hundreds of creative minds in India with innovative thinking engineers, managers, workers and supporting staff. Colleges should have an innovation centre to nurture innovative ideas and shape it into a product needed for customers. The innovation centre has to be led by creative leaders who can inspire the youth and the experienced to grow ideas into a product.

I have been presenting in many forums the pillars of the development profile of the nation by 2020. Let me present it to you:

- A nation where there is minimal rural and urban divide.
- A nation where there is an equitable distribution and adequate access to energy and quality water.
- A nation where agriculture, industry and service sector work together in symphony.
- A nation where education with a value system is not denied to any meritorious candidate because of societal or economic discrimination.

- A nation which is the best destination for the most talented scholars, scientists and investors.
- A nation where the best of healthcare is available to all.
- A nation where the governance is responsive, transparent and corruption free.
- A nation where poverty has been totally eradicated, illiteracy removed and crimes against women and children are absent and none in the society feels alienated.
- A nation that is prosperous, healthy, secure, devoid of terrorism, peaceful and happy and continues with a sustainable growth path.
- A nation that is one of the best places to live in and is proud of its leadership.

To achieve such a profile of India, we have the mission of transforming India into a developed nation. I believe there are five areas where India has great competence for integrated action. These are:

1. Agriculture and food processing
2. Reliable and quality electric power, surface transport and infrastructure for all parts of the country
3. Education and healthcare
4. Information and communication technology
5. Self-reliance in critical technologies.

These five areas are closely inter-related and if developed in a coordinated way, will lead to food, economic and national security.

In every domain, in every sector of the economy, whether it is science, engineering, technology, management, what is essential is the presence of creative leadership.

Let me connect how national economic development and creative leadership are related. The prosperity of the nation is empowered by economic development and great human character.

Here is how that can happen:

- A nation's economic development is powered by competitiveness.
- Competitiveness is powered by knowledge.
- Knowledge is powered by technology and innovation.
- Technology and innovation is powered by resource investment.
- Resource investment is powered by return on investment.
- Return on investment is powered by revenue.
- Revenue is powered by volume and repeat sales.
- Volume and repeat sales is powered by customer loyalty.
- Customer loyalty is powered by quality and value of products.
- Quality and value of products is powered by employee productivity and innovation.
- Employee productivity is powered by employee loyalty.
- Employee loyalty is powered by employee satisfaction.

- Employee satisfaction is powered by the working environment.
- Working environment is powered by management innovation.
- Management innovation is powered by creative leadership.

In my life, I have seen three dreams which have taken shape as vision, mission and realization. The space programme of the Indian Space Research Organization (ISRO), the AGNI programme of the Defence Research and Development Organization (DRDO) and Providing Urban Amenities in Rural Areas (PURA) mission becoming a national mission. Of course, these three programmes succeeded in the midst of many challenges and problems. I have worked in all these three areas. I want to convey to you what I have learnt on leadership from these three programmes:

- Leaders must have a vision.
- Leaders must have passion to realize the vision.
- Leaders must be able to travel into an unexplored path.
- Leaders must know how to manage success and failure.
- Leaders must have the courage to take decisions.
- Leaders should have nobility in management.
- Leaders should be transparent in every action.
- Leaders must work with integrity and succeed with integrity.

For success in all your missions, you have to become creative leaders. Creative leadership means exercising the vision to change the traditional role from the commander to the coach, manager to mentor, from director to delegator and from one who demands respect to one who facilitates self-respect. For a prosperous and developed India, the important thrust will be on the generation of a number of creative leaders from all our educational institutions, public organizations and the industry.

While we move towards a developed India, I believe that our inherent knowledge of healthy mind and body and the healing capacity is the most powerful resource we have for enhancing productivity, preventing disease, accelerating recovery from illness and injury, and maintaining well-being when disease cannot be cured. To heal, our bodies must be nourished and sheltered by the Earth, our minds and emotions must be awake and calm, and our social selves must reach out from need to service. Even when cures are not available, a form of healing can happen. And there is always a place for well-being. A culture that values wellness and healing will create a flourishing society—productive, creative, healthy and peaceful. Let us align our values with science and action to create policies and laws that promote flourishing; to link productivity and profit to health; to learn, play and entertain in celebration of collective well-being; and, to create a biomedical and healthcare system that heals as well as cures.

(from Address at the Mahindra Ecole College
of Engineering and to young engineers of
Tech Mahindra, Hyderabad, 14 May 2015)

Be the Unique You

History has proven that those who dare to imagine the impossible
are the ones who break all human limitations.

How many of my dear young friends feel confident that you will become a unique personality in whatever field you choose?

It is said, 'History has proven that those who dare to imagine the impossible are the ones who break all human limitations. In every field of human endeavour, whether science, medicine, sports, the arts, or technology, the names of the people who imagined the impossible are engraved in our history. By breaking the limits of their imagination, they changed the world.'

Let us study a few creative minds who made 'impossible' to 'possible' by their indomitable spirit. The story of human flight is nothing but the story of the creativity of the human mind and several struggles it undergoes to achieve excellence. In 1895, a great well-known scientist Lord Kelvin, who was the President of the Royal Society of London said, 'anything heavier than air cannot fly, and cannot be flown'. Within a decade, in 1903, the Wright brothers had proved that man could fly.

Von Braun, a very famous rocket designer, who built Saturn V to launch the capsule with astronauts and made moon walk a reality, said in 1975, 'If I am authorized, I will remove the word impossible.'

In ancient days, Ptolemaic astronomy was a widely used system in calculating the dynamics of various stars and planets.

The assumption then was that the Earth is flat. What a struggle scientists and astronomers had to do to prove that the Earth is spherical in shape and orbits the sun. The three great astronomers—Copernicus, Galileo and Kepler—had to give a new dimension to the world of astronomy. Today we take it for granted that Earth is a globe, orbiting around the sun, and the sun is in the Milky Way. All the technological advancements we have today are the outcome of scientific explorations of scientists of earlier centuries. At no time, was man beaten by problems. Then and now, he strives to continuously subjugate impossibility and succeed.

What lessons do we learn from all these achievements? According to the laws of aerodynamics the bumblebee should never be able to fly. Because of the size, weight and shape of its body in relationship to the total wing span, the flight of the bumblebee is scientifically impossible. But the bumblebee, being ignorant of scientific theory, goes ahead and flies anyway because it wants to fly. I would like the youth assembled here to take a lesson from these examples and work to make everything possible, because they are unique.

When I was the President of India, on 28 Aug 2006, I met a group of tribal students from Lead India 2020 movement. I asked all of them one question: 'What you want to become?' Out of many responses, one visually challenged boy studying in class nine got up. His name was Srikanth and he said to me, 'I will become the first visually challenged President of India.' I was very happy to see his vision and ambition. I firmly believe that small aim is a crime. I congratulated him and wished him well so he could realize his vision and told him to work hard for it.

He did work very hard and got 90 per cent in his tenth class and 96 per cent in the Intermediate. He had set a goal to study engineering in MIT, Boston USA. His relentless hard work not only secured him a seat there but he got full scholarship from the institute. Srikanth's achievement has inspired many to set ambitious goals for oneself. The training he took under the initiative of Lead India 2020 led him to set a high vision for himself. Seeing this impact of Lead India 2020 training, the movement and GE volunteers have funded Srikanth for his travel to USA. Today he is pursuing his studies at MIT, Boston. When GE offered him a job on the completion of his graduation, he told them that he would certainly come back to GE, if he couldn't become the President of India. What confidence that boy has amidst the difficulties and challenges in his life!

Recently, I had a chance to meet Srikanth and his teacher who brought him up at an interaction with physically challenged students organised by the Tamil Nadu government and Lead India 2020 at Coimbatore. He is doing fourth year in undergraduate studies in B.S. Computer Science and Management. Within this four years, he has started one company which produces consumer packaging items using bio-degradable materials. He has also been part of other social initiatives that he began while providing skill development training to the youth. At the meet, he gave an extempore speech on how to overcome disability and to have a strong mind and will power to overcome challenges. The message is, my young friends, it doesn't matter who you are, if you have a vision and determination to achieve that vision, you will certainly do so.

Here is another example of beautiful minds that are creative and with indomitable spirit.

This took place in Harali village, of Kolhapur district in Maharashtra where I met over 2,000 students hailing from different schools. When I was about to get down from the stage after finishing my lecture and interaction, a young boy of about eighteen years of age, held in the arms of his mother cried to meet me. I called both of them on to the stage. The polio affected boy could not walk, but he was strong in will power. He told me, 'My name is Shailesh and I am from this village Harali. You told us to have a dream. I am here to tell you my dream. I am a chess player. I will work very hard and some day I will become a Grandmaster.' I wished Shailesh all the best and said, 'You will succeed. Definitely, God is with you.' It is my unshakeable belief and my message to every young friend that will power can defeat any problem.

It is not only students but teachers too need to have creative and innovative minds in order to be effective. Teachers have to emerge as facilitators of new ideas and lead to lifelong innovative thinking in the young minds. This reminds me of a poem 'The Student's Prayer' by a Chilean biologist Maturana.

The Student's Prayer
Show me so that I can stand
On your shoulders.
Reveal yourself so that I can be
Something different.

Don't impose on me what you know,
I want to explore the unknown
And be the source of my own discoveries.
Let the known be my liberation, not my slavery.

(*from* Address and interaction with the students of
Shemford School, Dehradun, 29 April 2015)

What Can Science Give You?

Science gives you better eyes because science can remove mental limitations and challenge your brain to solve many problems that have puzzled the world for years.

Inventions and discoveries have emanated from creative minds that constantly work and create images of the outcome. With constant effort, all the forces of the universe work for that inspired mind, thereby leading to inventions or discoveries. So the higher the number of creative minds in a country, the faster it will transform into a developed nation.

Why is science important? What can science give you? And, what makes a scientist unique?

Friends, science gives you better eyes because science can remove the mental limitations and challenge your brain to solve many problems that have puzzled the world for years. Most of our friends, who are not in the field of science will slice time perhaps maximum up to one hundredth of a second. Scientists will slice time into femtoseconds (ten-fifteen seconds) which may decide a fast photochemical reaction. Few years back I saw a femtosecond laser at Maxivision Hospital, Hyderabad where precision eye surgery was being performed to remove the need for wearing spectacles.

When you think way back in time, there was the Big Bang, some 15,000 million years ago and then the beginning of life on Earth, about 3,800 million years ago. Science will connect you to the brains of many smart people who were there before you and who are performing some breath-taking research now.

It helps you stand on the shoulders of giants like Isaac Newton, who discovered the laws of gravitational force; Albert Einstein, who discovered of the general theory of relativity; Stephen Hawkings, the founder of string theory; Sir C.V. Raman, who discovered Raman effect; Chandrasekhar Subramanyam, who found the Chandra limit; Srinivasa Ramanujam, who thought of number theory; and James D. Watson, Francis Crick and Maurice Wilkins, who discovered the molecular structure of nucleic acids and its significance for information transfer in living material.

Science provides answers to challenging problems. Look at the southern sky with bright clouds lit by light. That is our galaxy; we belong to the Milky Way. Millions and millions of stars are there. We belong to a small star; what is that star? Our sun.

The solar system has eight planets. Our planet Earth has six billion people, and millions and millions of species. Can you imagine what science has revealed to all of us? Our galaxy and our sun and its characteristics have been identified. Our exact location with respect to the sun and in the galaxy has been discovered.

What have scientific discoveries led to? We know that Earth rotates on its own axis in 24 hours. We get day and night. How do you get the full moon night? Earth has its own satellite, the moon, which orbits around the planet Earth in 29 days. And how does the moon shine? Have you thought how do we get such beautiful light? How do we get the new moon? You all know it has been discovered. It is the dynamic movement of

Earth, sun and the moon in the space, which decides the full moon and the dark night.

The Earth system takes 365 days to orbit around the sun once. The sun itself orbits around our galaxy—the Milky Way. It is estimated that the sun takes 250 million years to orbit around the galaxy. All the astronomical discoveries have come out of science.

Now coming to the importance of looking after this Earth we have been given. You would have read in books and learnt from your teachers the process of photosynthesis in plants. 'When the sun shines, green plants breakdown water to get electrons and protons, use these particles to turn carbon dioxide into glucose and vent out oxygen as a waste product.' Each mature tree in a year absorbs 20 kg of carbon dioxide and transforms into wood and reinforces the branches of the tree. At the same time, it lets out into the atmosphere 14 kg of oxygen.

India's forests serve as a major sink of carbon dioxide. Our estimates show that the annual carbon dioxide removal by India's forests and tree cover is enough to neutralize 11.25 per cent of India's total greenhouse gas emissions. This is equivalent to offsetting 100 per cent emissions from all energy in residential and transport sectors or 40 per cent of the total emissions from agriculture sector (Source: India Forest and Tree Cover Contribution as Carbon Sink by Ministry of Environment and Forest). To augment this potential further, we should enhance the tree cover in addition to yearly plantation by the forest department. I urge every young friend to take this oath: 'I will plant ten trees and ensure their growth.'

For this unique contribution, Earth will be forever grateful.

(*from* Address at inauguration of science exhibition,
Ankleshwar, Gujarat, 24 April 2015)

Empowerment of
Three Billion People

When you are inspired by some great purpose, some extraordinary project, all your thoughts break their bounds.

Friends, excellence is not by accident. It is a process, where an individual, (or organization or nation) continuously strives to better himself. The performance standards are set by themselves, they work on their dreams with focus and are prepared to take calculated risks and do not get deterred by failures as they move towards their dreams. Then they step up their dreams as they tend to reach the original targets. They strive to work to their potential, and in the process they increase their performance thereby multiplying further their potential and this is an unending cycle.

Based on my own personal experiences, teachers provide not just curriculum based knowledge to pass examinations. They trigger life missions; they guide students to a value system.

Many of you have heard about the precise launch of the fourth Indian Regional Navigation Satellite, IRNSS-1D on 28 March 2015 by Polar Satellite Launch Vehicle, PSLV-C27 in its twenty-eighth consecutively successful mission. In a few weeks, this satellite, along with its three predecessors will form the backbone of an independent regional satellite system of India. It will provide accurate position information service to users in India as well as surrounding region extending upto 1,500 km from its boundary.

I would also like to refer to a significant event that happened on 18 December 2014. It was the suborbital experimental mission of ISRO's new generation launch vehicle GSLV Mark III. The experimental mission tested the vital atmospheric ascent of the new vehicle. It also injected the Crew Module CARE (Crew Atmospheric Re-entry Experiment) at an altitude of 126 km. Later the crew module was successfully recovered through operations from the Bay of Bengal. This mission paves the way for a new generation launch vehicle in a few years and very early initial engineering steps for developing Indian capability for human space missions. Some of you may have dreams of flying and you will be following such developments happening in our country and elsewhere. Depending on your interests, you may also keep abreast of developments in other areas of human endeavours in energy, water, agriculture, infrastructure development, social entrepreneurship.

Excellence and inquisitiveness about future technologies can be fostered by dynamic colleges. These are the eight aspects or characteristics of such institutions:

1. A college that radiates greatness by the teaching capacity of the teachers and how students are encouraged to walk with teachers.
2. A college is great because it cherishes the learning environment with library, Internet, e-learning and creative laboratories.
3. A college is great because it creates and generates students with confidence who feel 'I can do it' that in turn generates

a team spirit that says 'We will do it' and 'India will do it'.

4. A college that promotes all-round learning in all the students. Students stand on the shoulders of great teachers.

5. A college is great because it has teachers who lead a unique way of life with purity and become role models for the students and develop them as enlightened citizens.

6. A college is great because it has the capacity to teach all students to succeed.

7. A college that generates creativity among all students irrespective of whether they belong to arts or science stream.

8. A college is great when it generates alumni who cherish that they belong to this college.

The challenge of empowering 3 billion population of the world has multiple dimensions. Let us discuss four major such trends which will emerge and need to addressed:

i) New Consumption: If growth and development is to reach the world's population, it will bring about a colossal shift in the consumption patterns, pushing new demands for products so far unknown to half of humanity. For example, the current consumer expenditure per capita is about $800 for India, $1500 for China and $6,000 for Brazil. Compared to that, the same figure for USA stands at $35,000 per capita and for UK it is about $22,000. It is further estimated that a person born in 2009 in emerging economies will consume roughly 35 times more in real terms than a person born in 1979. This is bound to create a demand for fresh set of products and services which suit the local needs and context and multinationals will face stiff competition from smaller but local players. This will also include human development sectors such as education and healthcare where we are already seeing rise of distance learning, non-cognitive abilities and generic medicines.

Empowerment of three billion needs to be innovative to suit local contexts and communities.

ii) Energy: Development is a direct function of energy and as societies are empowered their demand for energy is bound to escalate. Global energy demand is expected to go up by 44 per cent by 2030. India's own power consumption is expected to treble to over 600 GW and China is expected to consumer over 1600 GW by 2030.

This is going to be met with shrinking natural resources such as fossil fuels including coal and petroleum. The emphasis has to shift towards new and renewable sources such as nuclear, especially thorium, wind, solar, geothermal, hydrogen fuels, biofuels and tidal power. Global societies need to realize that the energy sources of yesterday are simply not going to work in the future.

Empowerment of three billion needs to create new avenues to meet global energy demand.

iii) Environment: It is well established that the ways of the currently developed societies are unsustainable for the planet Earth. In fact, our estimates indicate that if all the three billion underprivileged are made to live at the same level as the currently developed societies, we would need roughly six new planet Earths to meet the resources needed and absorb the waste generated.

Even today, we are generating over 30 billion tones of carbon dioxide in the atmosphere, and it is expected that if current trends continue Earth would be irreversibly harmed beyond the year 2030.

Empowerment of three billion needs to be conscious of the impact on the environment.

iv) Social Conflicts: Driven by increasing economic gaps, fundamentalism, resource quests or historic differences, there has been a steady increase in global conflicts since the Second World War. While the number of inter-state conflicts has been relatively constant since 1946, the number of civil conflicts has risen by about three times, consuming large amounts of resources and bringing great loss of lives, especially in the developing world. The 300 richest people in the world command more wealth than the bottom 3 billion people. Equity in opportunity, basic human development for all and conflict resolution mechanism at local levels is the need of the hour.

Empowerment for three billion needs to be equitable, just and create opportunities for everyone.

Let me recall Maharishi Patanjali, who said 2,500 years ago: 'When you are inspired by some great purpose, some extraordinary project, all your thoughts break their bounds. Your mind transcends limitations, your consciousness expands in every direction, and you find yourself in a new, great and wonderful world. Dormant forces, faculties and talents come alive, and you discover yourself to be a greater person by far than you ever dreamt yourself to be.'

(*from* Address at Vijaya College, Bangalore, 30 March 2015)

Be the Change

Discover yourself to be a greater person by far than you ever dreamt yourself to be.

Dear friends, I strongly feel that no youth today needs to fear about the future. Why? The ignited mind of the youth is the most powerful resource on the Earth.

Let me give you some examples of those who made a change in their lives and became true ignited minds.

A unique experience happened when I went to Madurai to inaugurate the Paediatric Oncology Cancer unit at Meenakshi Mission Hospital on 7 January 2011. After I completed the task, suddenly one person from the audience approached me and his face looked familiar. When he came closer, I found out that he was once my driver when I was the Director of Defence Research and Development Lab (DRDL) at Hyderabad in 1982–92. His name is V. Kathiresan, and he had worked with me day and night for those ten years. During that time, I noticed, he was always reading some books, newspapers and journals during his waiting time in the car. That dedication had attracted me and I asked him a question. 'Why do you read during your leisure time?' He replied that his children used to ask him lot of questions. Since he didn't always know the answer, he would study whenever time permitted in order to give them the best answers. The spirit of learning in him impressed me and I told him to study formally through distance education and gave him some free time to attend the course and complete his 10+2 and then to apply for higher education. He took that as a challenge and kept on studying and upgraded his educational qualifications. He did B.A. (History), then he did M.A. (History) and then he did M.A. (Political Science) and completed his B.Ed and then M.Ed and he worked with me up to 1992. Thereafter he registered for his doctoral studies and got his PhD in 2001. He joined the Education Department of Tamil Nadu government and served there for a number of years. In 2010, he became an assistant professor in the Government Arts College at Mellur near Madurai.

When I was invited to address the students of UPMS School, Kovilpatti, I again met Professor Kathiresan who was sitting on the dais. I introduced Professor Kathiresan to the gathering and brought out how he, a native of that same town, has transformed himself, earned a doctorate and was teaching in a college after two decades of hard work. This incident cheered the entire young audience.

Friends, I visualize a scene. A school having about 50 teachers and 750 students. It is a place of beauty and for fostering creativity and learning. How is it possible? It is because the school management and the Principal selected the teachers who love teaching, who treat the students as their children or grandchildren. The children see the teachers as role models not only in teaching but how they conduct their lives.. Above all, I see an environment in which there is nothing like a good student, average student or poor student. The whole school and teacher system is involved in generating students who perform to their best. And above all, what should be the traits the teacher should possess based on teachers' life both inside the class room and outside the school? When good teachers walk among them, the students should feel the heat of knowledge and the purity of their lives radiate from them. This race of teachers should multiply.

As a child moves towards teenage and then adulthood, his carefree attitude is slowly taken over by many pressures. What will I do after my education? Will I get a proper employment?

Teachers and parents should preserve the happy smiles on the faces of their children even when they complete their school education. The student should feel confident that 'I can do it'. He or she should have the self-esteem and the capability to become an employment generator. This transformation can only be brought about by a teacher who has the vision to transform.

I have always liked to sit in a class. When I visit schools and colleges in India and abroad, I like to see how teachers teach and students interact in the classroom. Recently, I was in Andhra Pradesh, in a one-teacher school classroom. The school had classes only up to the fifth grade. I was with the students and the teacher was teaching. How happy were the children? The teacher was telling the young students, 'Dear children, you see the full moon, the beautiful scene in the sky brings smiles and cheers. Remember, as you smile the family also smiles. How many of you keep your parents happy?' The whole class lifted their hands. They said, they would do it. I also lifted my hand along with the students.

Another experience was during my visit to UAE. I inaugurated an Indian school in Dubai. When the preparation was going on for the inaugural function, I was moving from place to place in the school. I visited classrooms where students from class five and six were being taught. As soon as the teacher saw me, she asked me to take the class. So I started interacting with the students. Instead of loading them with the lessons. I asked them how many planets does our sun have? Many hands went up. One girl said, there are nine planets and some students said, there are eight planets. I said the right answer is eight planets, since the ninth planet Pluto has been removed from the list of planets, because it does not meet the criteria of a planet, in size, weight and orbital motion. I asked, 'Tell me, which is our planet?' There was a chorus in reply, 'Earth'. Then I asked, 'Who will talk about the Earth?' One sixth class student got up and said, 'Our Earth rotates on its own axis.' Many students said, 'It takes 24 hours for one orbit that's how we get day and night.' I was very pleased with the knowledge of the young on the solar system. Then I asked the class, what does the Earth do, there was pin drop silence. Again a fifth class student said, 'Earth orbits around the sun.' How much time it takes to complete the one orbit? Many hands went up, they said 365 days. Our sun belongs to which galaxy? Only one boy responded, 'Milky Way'. How much time our sun takes for one orbit of our galaxy? No response. Of course, it is difficult. I gave the answer: 200 million years. The children had a great surprise. I was impressed with the class and greeted them and left.

I am giving you these examples to illustrate, how students can be encouraged to build their self-confidence. I am sure teachers may adopt several methods to make the class dynamic and creative for promoting sustained interest among the students.

(*from* Address at Villa Nazreth English Medium School and other schools, Aryanad, Thiruvananthapuram, 22 February 2015 and Address and interaction with the students of CRPF Public School, Hakimpet, Telangana, 20 March 2015)

Striving for Excellence

Excellence happens not by accident. It is a process.

Creativity comes from beautiful minds. Creative minds have the ability to imagine or invent something new by combining, changing or reapplying existing ideas. A creative person accepts change and a willingness to play with ideas and possibilities, a flexibility of outlook, the habit of enjoying the good, while looking for ways to improve it. The important aspect of creativity is seeing the same thing as everybody else, but thinking of something different. Innovation and creativity ultimately lead to a culture of excellence.

Excellence in thinking and action is the foundation for any mission. What is excellence? Friends, you all belong to the youth community, which should stand for a culture of excellence. Moreover, excellence is not by accident. It is a process, where an individual or organization or nation continuously strives to better oneself.

Sometime back, I was going through an article which was about the top science advancements in the year 2014. I came across many cases, and most of them were directly benefiting human health, education, safety and energy. Let me share three such major breakthroughs.

We are very close to finding a cure for diabetes using human embryonic stem cells technologies.

As you may know, beta cells in pancreas produce insulin

and the destruction of these cells causes Type I diabetes. But so far the efforts to turn embryonic stem cells into beta cells proved to be 'frustratingly slow'. In 2014, two studies showed that enough beta cells can be produced in less than two months to replace the beta cells in the body. Of course, before being used, the why beta cells die in the body has to be identified. But scientists are confident that we will soon finally find a permanent cure for diabetes.

Let me discuss a second event which is a convergence between space sciences and traction and rocketry technologies. In 2014, for the first time ever in the history of mankind, a man-made object landed on a comet. The Rosetta spacecraft finally reached the 67p Churyumov-Gerasimenko comet, its destination, after travelling 6.4 billion km and a chase of ten years, since it was launched by the European Space Agency (ESA). Rosetta deployed its probe, Philae. The comet has quite a low bulk density, something in the region of 300 kg per cubic metre, which means that if you put the object in an ocean, it would float.

Though the landing was soft, Philae came to rest on its side and a bit off the actual landing spot, in the shadow of a cliff and went to rest as its batteries could not be charged. But it did manage to send some vital data.

Nearly 80 per cent of scientific data is expected to come from Rosetta that reached the comet and has been orbiting it since then. It is orbiting at an altitude of 10 km from the comet's surface, and has already transmitted massive amounts of data. This could perhaps be our future of exploring deep space and combating the dangers of meteor strikes on Earth.

The third event is related to computer science and neurology. In 2014, computer engineers at IBM and other companies took a leaf out of how the human brain works and designed neuromorphic chips that can process information in a manner similar to the human brain. This means that they work unlike today's computers that carry out logical operations but struggle to 'integrate vast amounts of data'. Our brains don't face that difficulty. We seamlessly integrate vast amount of data collected from diverse sources to build the final product. This becomes possible as individual neurons communicate with their neighbours to enable parallel data processing.

The new chip with a brain-inspired computer architecture powered by an unprecedented 1 million neurons and 256 million synapses—TrueNorth—mimics the brain but at very small scale with 5.4 billion transistors and 256 million 'synapses'. The brain has 100 billion neuron cells and 100 trillion synapses. It only consumes 70mW during real-time operation—orders of magnitude less energy than traditional chips.

Science thrives when it converges to solve pressing challenges of the world and this is the 21st century requirement from engineers.

(*from* Address at College of Engineering, Trivandrum, 23 February 2015)

Books as Our Guides

Coming into contact with a good book and possessing it, is indeed an everlasting enrichment.

I had a mission of meeting the young and sharing their thoughts and their dreams. I have so far met about 19.5 million youth in the last two decades. What did I learn from these meetings and what is my message to the youth?

I would like to share an experience which I had in the year 2010. I was taking a class of 72 students both graduate and post graduate at the Gatton College of Business and Economics, Lexington, USA. We used to have thirty minutes earmarked for discussions in every class.

One day, a course participant, Stephanie, who was a school teacher before joining the course, asked me an unusual question. She asked, 'Dr Kalam, yesterday night I was reading one of your books. You have done many tasks, so tell us what one task gave you the most bliss?'

Let me share my answer with all of you.

When we launched the first indigenous satellite launch vehicle SLV-3 in 1980, it gave me lot of happiness. When AGNI reached the target at 2,000 km in 1989, it gave me different kind of happiness. When our team successfully tested a nuclear weapon at the 52 degree centigrade heat in Pokhran desert in western India in 1998, it gave me great joy. When our team prepared the Vision 2020 document for transforming the nation into an economically developed nation, it gave me a good sense of happiness. Then Stephanie reminded me, 'But what gave you bliss?'

I told her, that I was getting to the real answer. The experience that gave me the greatest bliss was when I played a part in creating lightweight callipers to be worn by children afflicted by polio. The removal of the pain and the freedom attained by the children gave me a state of bliss, which I never experienced during any other achievement in my life.

I have also attained bliss while reading some good books and understanding the depths of meaning in their pages. Coming into contact with a good book and possessing it, is indeed an everlasting enrichment. Books become permanent companions. Sometimes, they are born before us; they guide us during our life journey and continue for many generations. I had bought a book titled *Light from Many Lamps* in the year 1953 from an old book store in Moore Market, Chennai. This book remained my close friend and also companion for more than five decades. The book was so used it had to be bound many times. Whenever there is a problem, the book wipes away the tears based on the experience of great minds. When happiness overwhelms, the book again softly touches the mind and brings about a balanced thinking. I have realized the importance of the book again, when a friend of mine who is in the judiciary presented me with the new edition of the same book in the year 2004. He told me the best thing he can give me was this book. Maybe fifty years from now the same book may take a new avatar. Basically books are eternal.

On 11 August 2009, I was participating in the valedictory

function of the book fair festival at Erode (Tamil Nadu). While addressing the audience, I suggested that every one of the participants of the book fair to allocate at least one hour in a day for reading quality books. This will enrich them with knowledge to empower the children and see them grow as great children. I also suggested all the parents should start a small library in their own home with approximately 20 books to begin with. This library should have ten children's books, so that the children in the house can also cultivate a reading habit at an early age looking at the parents reading quality books. Many people who attended this function appreciated this thought and they immediately started a library at their homes. I administered the following oath to the participants:

Today onwards, I will start a home library with 20 books out of which ten books will be children's books.

My children will enlarge this home library to make it 200 books.

My grandchildren will lead a great home library of 2,000 books.

I consider our library is a lifelong treasure and the precious property of our family.

We will spend at least one hour at the home library to study along with our family members.

After taking the oath on home library, a surprising event happened at the end of the meeting. Thousands and thousands people rushed to the bookstalls and within an hour most of the books at the book fair had been sold out.

Please remember, a home library is the greatest wealth.

Reading for one hour each day in the home library will transform into children into great teachers, great leaders, great intellectuals, great engineers, great scientists. Each one of you can consider creating a home library which will enable the entire family to discuss common topics during dinner time every day. Apart from enriching the knowledge of every family member this reading habit creates a healthy discussion among the family members, which is essential for the sustained harmony of the entire family.

(*from* Address at the Jaipur Literature Festival,
24 January 2015)

A Book in Every Hand

We must transcend barriers of language, distance, cost and even reading ability to make books reach every person.

Dear friends, India has embarked on the mission of skilling 500 million people by the year 2022. These 500 million people, mostly youth will need to be empowered with knowledge from books and journals. Hence the role of libraries is very important in this domain. How can we enhance the reach of libraries?

One possible way is to integrate the existing libraries with mobile platforms and enable mobile libraries. India has over 700 million mobile subscribers. We can create mobile-based books, which can be shared by mobile libraries across the nation. Moreover, with more number of translations and processing power available in mobile phones, we can develop real time translation facilities by which any book can be translated in any language by the mobile application itself. We can also enable audio in these books, so that people with visual impairment or limited reading ability can access the wealth of books and libraries. In this way, we can truly transcend barriers of language, distance, cost and even reading ability and make books reach every person.

A book which I have cherished is *Man, The Unknown* by Dr Alexis Carrel, a doctor-turned-philosopher and a Nobel Laureate. This book highlights how the mind and body have to be treated together as the two are integrated. You cannot treat one and ignore the other. In particular, children who dream of becoming doctors should read this book. They will learn that the human body is not a mechanical system; it is a very intelligent organism with a most intricate and sensitive feedback system. The human system is an integrated life package made of psychological and physiological systems.

I venerate Thiruvalluvar's *Thirukkural*, which provides an excellent code of conduct for life and the author's thoughts that go beyond a nation, beyond languages, beyond religion, and beyond culture indeed elevates the human mind. I would like to recall one couplet from *Thirukkural* which has influenced my life for the last six decades. It says that whatever may be the depth of the river or lake or pond, whatever may be the condition of the water, the lily flower always blossoms. Similarly, if there is a definite determination to achieve a goal even if it is impossible to achieve, the person succeeds.

Let me now tell you how an autobiography of a village boy enriched my thinking on laser technology.

In 1968, an Indian scientist, a PhD in physics from IIT, Kharagpur and hailing from rural West Bengal was invited to join the team at the Research and Technology Center of Northrop Corporation, a major aerospace contractor who offered extraordinary facilities for a physicist. He was working in the area of carbon monoxide (CO) laser. Based on his research, in 1968, his colleagues at Northrop demonstrated the most powerful continuous laser to date. In a further step forward, the Indian scientist was able to make the laser operate at room temperatures, something previously thought impossible.

The Indian scientist presented his results at a seminar at the University of California, Los Angeles. Edward Teller, the man whose revelatory insights had earned him the title 'Father of the H-Bomb' was there. Dr Teller was so intrigued by the presentation by the Indian scientist that when he felt nature's call and had to leave the room, he requested the scientist to suspend the talk till he returned. Later, a Soviet scientist wrote in a prestigious Russian journal, 'After Bhaumik's thorough work on the CO laser, there isn't much left to do (on that laser).' This brought international recognition to this scientist. Do you know who is the scientist about whom I am talking? It is Dr Mani Lal Bhaumik who has authored a book titled *Code Name God* where he shows the connections between science and spirituality. I read the book in one sitting and really enjoyed every chapter which brings out the pain and pleasure of the life of Dr Bhaumik. I am sure, all of you will be keen to read more about this laser scientist. His invention in laser has led to the development of LASIK, an important application of eye surgery.

Now I would like to share with you a real life story which happened two decades ago in Honolulu. This incident I read in the book titled *Everyday Greatness* written by Steven R. Covey.

Lindy Kunishima and Geri had two daughters Trudi, thirteen, and Jennifer, nine, and a small son Steven. At the age of eighteen months, Geri detected something abnormal about his son. A CT scan by a neurologist revealed that the vermis, an area of the brain that transmits messages to and from the body's muscles, had not developed. The neurologist declared that, Steven will never walk or talk, or do anything that requires muscle control and he would be profoundly challenged mentally and physically. Geri couldn't eat or sleep for days. But Trudi challenged the doctor's prognosis and announced that, 'she did not believe what the doctor said about Steven and took a note that she will work till Steven became normal.' They started reading a passage to him everyday on the dinner table which became a habit. Jennifer and Trudi also asked questions and pointed out animals or people illustrated in the hooks. For many weeks there was no response from Steven.

After three months, one evening Steven suddenly wriggled away from the cushions. The family watched him inching towards the children's books. Steven flipped through the book till he saw the page filled with pictures of animals. The following night, as Jennifer prepared to read, her brother crawled to the same book and opened the same page again. This showed that Steven had a memory which was continuously improving.

Both Trudi and Jennifer played the piano in the presence of Steven. One day after practicing, Jennifer lifted Steven from his place under the piano. This time, he was uttering a new sound. He was humming the music. Simultaneously, the family also worked to build up his muscles through massages. Geri, Trudi and Jennifer dabbed peanut butter on the boy's lips, and by licking it off, he exercised his tongue and jaw. When Steven was four and a half years old, he still couldn't speak words, but he could make some sounds and he had a remarkable memory. After studying a 300-piece jigsaw puzzle, he could assemble the pieces in one sitting.

After many rejections, Steven was admitted in a pre-school

by Louise Bogart of Robert Allen Montessori School who found that Steven was determined to make himself understood.

One day, Bogart stood off to the side and was watching the teacher work with another child on numbers. 'What number comes next?' the teacher asked. The child drew a blank. 'Twenty!' Steven blurted. Bogart's head swivelled. Steven had not only spoken clearly, but also given the correct answer. Bogart approached the teacher. 'Did Steven ever work on this?' she asked. 'No,' the teacher answered. 'We worked with him a lot on numbers from one through ten. But we didn't know he had learned any beyond ten.' Bogart told his mother that, 'This is just the beginning of what the Steven is capable of.' His motor skills remained poor, so Jennifer, Geri, and Trudi worked hard at making his written scrawl legible. 'I can do it,' Steven assured Jennifer one day. 'Just give me time.'

After that, Steven continuously improved and was admitted to a mainstream Catholic school in 1990. Such is the power of collective determination to cure a child.

> (*from* Inaugural address at National Convention on
> Knowledge, Library and Information Networking,
> Puducherry, 9 December 2014)

Transforming the Future

As you grow up, you will have the challenges and opportunities for solving many problems faced by humanity.

I see in my young friends some who will be astronauts and be amongst the first to set foot on the planet Mars and even beyond—like Titan the moon of Saturn. You may be the first human to find other planets for us to live and create the first outer planet liveable zones. I see in you, friends, unique scientists in genetics who will cure diseases which have affected us for centuries. Some of you may even give to the world the solution on how to immunize humans from all forms of diseases. My discussion here hence will be for future transformers of human civilization.

As you hear about scientific challenges for the future, as you discuss with scientists your dreams, please keep one message clear, our utmost priority is how to use science and technology for the betterment of human lives and the Earth.

I recall when I was in Beijing, the capital of China in 2014, the city was getting ready to receive world leaders for the APEC (Asia Pacific Economic Cooperation) Summit 2014 which was being organized there. What the students shared with me was interesting information—the government had taken a decision to allow only half the cars on the road because the pollution levels in the city were too high.

Of course, the Chinese government can simply order and do it, which would be difficult for a democracy like ours to follow. But, the point I am making here is that most of the pollution happens due to motor vehicles of various types that use fossil fuel. Only solution for India is to go for cleaner fuel options like electric cars or fully electric public transport vehicles.

Every year, the factories which give out smoke and ash, the cars which burn fuel and other human activities generates more than 30 billion tonnes of carbon dioxide. This is injected into the atmosphere and causes global warming, rising sea levels and polar ice cap melting as you all know. The youth will have to find solutions for this.

My visualization of human civilization by the year 2050 for a prosperous and peaceful globe is like this:

1. Every citizen will have access to adequate quantity and quality water for consumption, sanitation and irrigation.
2. Agriculture will enable constant renewal and enrichment of the soil.
3. There will be an adequate access to energy to all in the world and it will be based on green sources.
4. Information and communication technology will penetrate and enable every field of human endeavour.
5. Education will be the tool by which science and technology will be delivered to all, leading to the birth of the global knowledge society backed by value system and a spirit of compassion.
6. Healthcare will witness an emphasis on preventive healthcare and tailored medical treatments for each individual leading to a disease free society with increased longevity.

7. Minimum guaranteed quality of life will be ensured to every global citizen.
8. Global Green House Gas Equilibrium will be achieved and the risk of climate change will be eliminated.
9. Human habitation will be extended to beyond Earth. Multidisciplinary global leaders will emerge with a vision for sustainable development

It is estimated that the population of India by 2050 will be one-fifth of the global population. Hence, our role in the achievement of these visions for the human civilization will be important and others will have to follow.

Friends, as you grow up, you will have the challenges and opportunities for solving many problems faced by humanity as well as discovering new phenomena in outer space or under the sea. You will also have challenges in bringing back a clean environment by replacing fossil fuels with renewable energy from sun, wind etc. The following are some typical great challenges, as we foresee today:

1. Increasing the agriculture production from the existing 200 million tonne to 340 million tonne with reduced land availability from 170 to 100 hectares, reduced water availability and reduced number of people working in farming.
2. Evolution of clean atmosphere by replacing fossil fuels by cost effective renewable energy systems.
3. Exploring the human body, particularly gene characterization through the proteomics project for developing gene-based drugs.

4. Accurate weather prediction and earthquake prediction
5. Evolution of multimedia application for meeting the communication needs using high bandwidth mobile wireless.
6. Evolution of unified field theory which may be the ultimate of physics revealing how the universe is born and how we are born.
7. Evolution of habitats outside Earth and to bring back to Earth new material like helium 3, and also create alternative habitats and means of generation of solar power.

(*from* Address at the inauguration of 102nd National Children's Science Congress, Mumbai, 4 January 2015)

Intellect and Empathy

Youth has got the power of ideas, ambition and ability.

As you all know the Mars Orbiter Mission was successfully inserted into the Martian orbit on 24 September 2014. My friends at ISRO told me that all the five scientific payloads were switched on and the health of the spacecraft is normal including high voltages on two of the payloads. The Mars colour camera has been sending pictures of Mars which are of very good resolution. Most of the earlier high resolution images of Mars were put together to give a picture of the complete disc. ISRO's camera has a large field of view of about 5 degree by 5 degree and it can get the complete disc picture with high resolution. You can see these pictures on ISRO's Facebook and Twitter pages.

I asked my ISRO friends, did they have any issues with the Mars Orbiter Mission? They told one particular incident. During the passage of Comet C/2013 A1 the spacecraft had to be shielded. To do this, the spacecraft and subsystems were protected by tuning the orbit such that the spacecraft was behind the planet Mars during the passage of the comet. All subsystems continued to function normally. The lesson here is that scientific minds need to be innovative and prepared to handle any unknown difficulty in their missions.

The nation needs ignited minds of the youth.

When I was a young boy of your age, I had few concerns

in my life. Will I ever go out of my village for high school studies? When I reached the high school in small town and saw my colleagues well dressed, speaking good English, I used to ask myself, when will I enter their company? When I reached ninth standard I had a concern, will I get good marks to go for higher education particularly engineering science or medicine? When I reached tenth class all these concerns vanished because of the company of a great teacher. He gave me the vision for my life. My teacher's name was Sivasubramania Iyer. Definitely your schools will have great teachers who will help you realize your vision for the future. Along with those who understand and inspire you, always make sure to have the company of good books and great minds.

For a happy and peaceful society, each citizen of the nation has to be facilitated to develop two unique traits. One is intellect and the other is empathy. This can be acquired through good parents, good teachers, good books and being in the company of great people. If this is not done at the right age, human beings can become a Shaitan (devil) particularly if the intellect acts without empathy. We as a nation, have to take this message and develop our youth with these traits. Thinking of a good human being, I am reminded of the story of Imam Ghazali. That was narrated to me by my father when I was fifteen years old.

Imam Ghazali was a saint teacher who lived in the twelfth century. My father narrated to me story where Imam Ghazali was tested by Shaitan, the transgressed Angel. One day, Imam Ghazali was unfolding his prayer mat for Magrib Namaz. At that time, the Shaitan appeared in front of him and said, 'Respected

Imam Sahib, I am just now coming from heaven where there was a discussion about great human beings and you have been judged as the best human being living on Earth. As a recognition of your great stature, you have been exempted from the trouble of performing namaz in future.'

Imam Ghazali was restless as the namaz time was approaching. So he looked at Shaitan and said, 'Shaitan Sahib, first of all performing namaz is not a trouble at all and when even Prophet Mohammed (peace be upon him), was not exempted from performing namaz five times a day, how can a poor imam like me be exempted?' He went on to perform the namaz. When he completed the namaz, Imam Ghazali saw Shaitan was still standing in front of him. Imam Sahib asked him what he was waiting for. Shaitan said, 'O Imam, you have excelled even the most favoured Prophet Adam, who could not win over my deception and I made him eat the forbidden fruit.' Realizing that Shaitan was flattering him, Imam Sahib prayed to Allah, 'Oh Almighty, help me and save me from the deception of flattery.' This made the disappointed Shaitan finally disappear. His mission failed. But one of the great human beings succeeded.

Friends, what is the message from this story? We not only have to develop intellect and empathy, but must also guard against temptations while contributing towards societal missions. Our own Father of the Nation has set many examples in accounting even a paisa of public money and working with commitment to bring about peace and prosperity of the nation.

I suggest that teachers ensure that the youth have three unique qualities of life:

1. Realizing the importance of the present, that is, today.
2. Building confidence so students believe 'I can do it'.
3. Building righteousness in the heart.

India today has a mission of transforming itself into a developed nation with a strong value system. This is a great challenge. This can be achieved through our youth power. Youth has got the power of ideas, ambition and ability. This resource of the youth is an important building block for transforming India into a developed nation.

If you have an aim in life, continuously acquire the knowledge, work hard with confidence to win and have the confidence to defeat problems and succeed with a righteous heart, you will definitely succeed in all your missions. It does not matter who you are.

My best wishes to all of you for success in your life's missions.

(*from* Address to the students of Angul, Odisha, 29 November 2014)

From Child to Leader

A leader says, 'What can I do for you?'

would like to talk today about the role of a teacher.

I have interacted with more than 20 million school children and millions of teachers across the globe. Wherever I go, be it India, China, UK or any part of world, the voice of the youth is unique and strong in articulating their vision and dream and they are willing to work for it. Everyone dreams of living in a prosperous nation, a happy nation, a peaceful nation and a safe nation. Prosperity, happiness and peace always have to come together. When all three of them converge, then a nation will truly be a Developed Nation.

Children work in the school for about 25,000 hours during the twelve years of primary and secondary education. Teachers of excellence, with their experience, can become role models to the students. I will be discussing the capacities to be created in the children by the school.

Every one of us has gone through the various phases of education from childhood to profession. Please visualize a scene—a child, a teenager, an adult and a leader. How does each one react to a particular situation? The situation is human need. The child asks, 'What can you do for me?' The teenager says, 'I want to do it alone.' The young person proclaims, 'Let us do it together.' The leader offers, 'What can I do for you?'

So, the teachers have got a tremendous responsibility to

transform a child into a leader, the transformation of 'what can you do for me' to 'what can I do for you'. That will demand a teacher to be a visionary with an ability to inspire. Also, the teachers has to impart learning to the children in such a way as to bring out the best in them. The best in students emerges by the integrated influence of teachers.

As young students, I had the opportunity at St. Joseph's College in southern India to witness a scene. A unique, divine looking personality was walking through the college campus every morning teaching mathematics to B.Sc. (Honours) and M.A. (Mathematics) students. Young students looked at him with awe and respect. He was a personality symbolizing our own culture. When he walked, knowledge radiated all around. The great personality was Professor Thothatri Iyengar, the great teacher. At that time, Calculus Srinivasan was my mathematics teacher. Calculus Srinivasan used to talk about Professor Thothatri Iyengar with deep respect. During those days, he and Professor Iyengar had an understanding to have an integrated class by ProfessorIyengar for first year B.Sc. (Hons) and first year B.Sc. (Physics). I had the opportunity to attend his classes, particularly on the subjects of modern algebra, statistics and also once I heard him teaching complex variables. When we were in the B.Sc. first year, Calculus Srinivasan used to select top ten students for the Mathematics Club of St. Joseph's, where Prof. Iyengar used to give lecture series. One day, in 1952, I still remember, he gave a one-hour lecture on ancient mathematicians and astronomers of India and introduced three great mathematicians and astronomers. He spoke for nearly one hour. The lecture still rings in my ears.

I was introduced to the pride of the nation: pioneers in astronomy and mathematics Aryabhata, Bhaskara and Ramanujam who gave to the world the zero, computed the orbit period of the Earth around the sun and discovered many stunning concepts in number theory. These incidents and knowledge became the foundation for my education, learning with hope and value system. My teachers of primary, secondary and college education had put me a few decades ahead. I am confident that there are many such teachers in the teaching profession today. In the education environment teachers need to ask, what kind of human beings do we want to make of ourselves? What capacities do we want to give our children? We want to give our children the capacity for contributing to economic development and nation building. How to achieve this? There are five areas for simultaneous development: financial investment, education and healthcare, information and communication technology, infrastructure development and self-reliance in critical technologies.

For achieving the above mission, the capacities required in schools and students are:

- The capacity for research or inquiry
- The capacity for creativity and innovation, particularly the creative transfer of knowledge
- The capacity to use high technology
- The capacity for entrepreneurial leadership
- The capacity for moral leadership

We have so far seen two dimensions of the world. The first one is about the stunning evolution of the human race, the technological marvels that have and continue to improve the quality of the world and the integration of global expertise that can enable fast technological progress of the society. The other dimension is the humongous challenges faced by humanity, particularly inequality. There are natural phenomena to be understood like earthquakes; there are several social factors to be tackled. However when you look at all issues in an integrated manner, you will agree that solutions lie in further linking society, technology and education. The current challenges need the application of science and technology for appropriate solutions. And that requires education that makes students appreciate the societal issues and technology requirements. Both the challenges of society and disciplines of technology are borderless. Hence education also has to have this characteristic.

I firmly believe that the approach of research-education-research is most vital. The teachers in academic educational institutions have to be enabled with time and resources to enable this. Professional institutions may be able to give a thrust in this direction in identifying areas of research, enabling factors, encouraging research publications, visibility of research in work environment and inculcating the idea of research mindset from pre-school level. They may bring out easily readable booklets on research topics and inspiration through example of great research pioneers and their work impacting social development.

There are a number of engineering colleges in the country and we come to know that several seats don't get filled. We also hear that when students come out of the college they do not get employment. The employing organizations frequently point out that the education they have received is not sufficient for employability.

On skill development also, on a day-to-day basis we hear that we do not have sufficiently skilled people in our villages and towns. So it is a paradoxical situation; while the society needs large number of people with engineering expertise and skill, in reality the output from educational institutions are said to be not up to the mark in many cases. And India has the largest youth power in the world. On the other hand, India needs large numbers of qualified manpower. There are two directions in which we have to work. One is the type of skills needed at various levels and impart them. We need to review the content of syllabus and provide sufficient time for this aspect. Professionals and institutions can play a good role in this. The skills to which the students are trained have to of global level. We also need to focus on imparting entrepreneurship to the young, so they become employment generators rather than employment seekers. In summary, the education strategy has to address societal challenges and technological advances and focus on research, skills, along with strong fundamentals in technology and communication skills.

If all the attributes are inculcated in a student, by the Principal, by the teacher, by the parents, then he or she will have a burning desire to learn throughout one's life and will also set an example for others. A perfect learner will not only learn from the classroom, but also from the environment. I firmly believe that the teachers' mission is to generate perfect learners.

What is the type of school that creates perfect learners?

Learning through enquiry or research using the latest technologies to acquire the information is important.

Creativity should flourish in the schools by students learning to teach themselves and by teaching other students.

The value of giving to others should be cultivated by asking the question how my learning can benefit others. How can I contribute to my own development and at the same time to the development of others and the nation?

For imbibing moral development, values such as team work, fair play, cooperation, doing things right and doing the right thing, hard work and commitment to a cause larger than oneself are to be emphasized, while keeping in mind our cultural fabric and our own value systems.

Friends, I am also a teacher and I work with teachers and students. Based on great teachers, I would like to share some thoughts on teachers' mission.

The teacher's task is to transform students to be creative and to excel. In their class, there is nothing like average students. Every student should reach the peak. The teacher's noble life becomes a message to the students.

(*from* Address and Interaction with principals and teachers of Indian schools at Indian School, Bahrain, 6 February 2015)

The Evolution of Creative Leaders

A leader should work with integrity and succeed with integrity.

My book *Ignited Minds* was born in 2001 out of my personal mission to 'ignite and nurture creative, ethical scientific minds that advance the human condition'. My professional responsibilities gave me opportunities to understand creative and evolving leadership traits at different levels for technology and missions. Biographies and articulation of world leaders, great philosophers and change makers have always been inspiring. When I was part of a national team for evolution of India's Vision 2020, the perception of leadership about technology, society and nation was illuminating. Interaction with youth and their focused questions on development made me further reflect on leadership traits. The presidency and thereafter gave me opportunities to interact with great leaders, nationally and globally. You would agree with me that perceptive creative leadership at functional, organizational, national and global levels is an essential component to realize the aspirations of humankind for peace and prosperity.

So how to evolve creative leadership? To start with, the following are traits of creative leadership:

- Envisioning
- Perceptive midcourse management
- Courage of conviction and compassion

- Foresight to anticipate social potential of a nascent technology and focus
- Scientific talent synthesised with farmers and administrators producing green revolution Institutional framework and organizational culture
- Life time mission in science
- Able and honest project administration

Let me begin with the experience of Mahatma Gandhi, the father of our nation. He led our nation to freedom from British rule using his innovative doctrine of non-violence (ahimsa). I had a unique experience, a few years back that reveals how a single leader can inspire a large population. I happened to meet, in Delhi, the grand-daughter of Mahatma Gandhi, Mrs Sumitra Kulkarni. She narrated to me an incident about her grandfather, which she personally witnessed.

Each day, as you all are aware, Gandhiji used to have prayer meetings at a fixed time in the evening. After the prayers, usually there would be a collection of voluntary gifts for the welfare of the needy. The followers used to collect whatever was given by the people of all sections and this collection was counted and accounted for by the supporting staff.

The collected amount would be informed to Gandhiji before his dinner. The next day, a bank man would come to take this money. Once, the bank man reported that there was a discrepancy of few paise in the money offered to him and the money collected. Gandhiji, on hearing this, went on a fast telling that this is a donation for the poor and we have to account for every paisa.

Dear friends, such an act of righteousness should be practiced by all of us. As managers and leaders of tomorrow all of you must dedicate yourselves to practice righteousness in all your thoughts and actions.

I recall my travelling on 16 September 2004 in a first class compartment in a train of 1900's vintage organized by Durban state of South Africa. When the train was moving from one station to another, Mahatma Gandhi's struggle against apartheid system in South Africa was going through my mind.

The train halted at Pietermartizburg, the station where the monster of apartheid bite Gandhiji on a cold winter night. He was evicted out of a first-class compartment because of the colour of his skin. When I alighted at the Pietermartizburg railway station, I saw a plaque on the railway station, which reads like this:

In the Vicinity of this plaque
M.K. GANDHI was evicted
from a first class
compartment on the night of
7 June 1893.
This incident changed
the course of his life.
He took up the fight
against racial oppression.
His active non-violence
started from that date.

This was the rebirth of Ahimsa dharma after the Kalinga War in 300 BC. Gandhiji later developed the Ahimsa dharma and gave India a powerful tool to win independence. He was influenced by Abraham Lincoln's Gettysburg speech. Teachings of Gandhi came to inspire non-violent movements notably in the U.S.A. under the civil rights leader Martin Luther King.

When I was standing at the Pietermartizburg railway station my thoughts were hovering on two scenes, which I experienced in South Africa. One scene was in Robben Island where Dr Nelson Mandela had been imprisoned for twenty-six years in a very small cell, and the other scene was at the house of Dr Nelson Mandela.

Cape Town is famous for its Table Mountain; it has got three peaks called Table Peak, Devil Peak and Fake Peak. Between the peaks it was a beautiful sight throughout the day, sometimes dark clouds and sometimes white clouds embracing the peaks. Table Mountain is very close to the Atlantic Ocean. I flew by helicopter to Robben Island from Cape Town in ten minutes. When we reached the Island, except the sea roaring, the whole island was silent. This was the place the freedom of individuals was chained. Mr Ahmed Kathrada, a South African, who was a co-prisoner with Dr Nelson Mandela, received us at the Island. What surprised me was seeing the tiny room where sleeping and all human needs had to be fulfilled. It has to be remembered that Dr Nelson Mandela, who was 6 feet tall was imprisoned in that room for twenty-six years—fighting against the apartheid. The major part of his life was spent in this silent island. He used to be taken for quarrying in the nearby mountain for a few hours in the bright sun. This was the time his sight got damaged. In spite of his body being tortured he revealed to the world his indomitable spirit. He evolved a manuscript of freedom in tiny letters every day, when the jail wardens went to sleep. This manuscript finally became the famous book *A Long Walk to Freedom.*

It was a great event for me to meet Dr Mandela in his house in Johannesburg. What a moving reception, the man at the age of eighty-six gave with all smiles. Dear friends, I would like to share with you, when I entered Dr Nelson Mandela's house, I saw his cheerfulness—this mighty man who got freedom for South Africa from the tyranny of apartheid.

When I was leaving he walked me out till the portico. While walking he discarded his walking stick and I became his support. While walking I asked him, 'Dr Mandela can you please tell me about the pioneers of anti-apartheid movement in South Africa?' He responded spontaneously, 'Of course one of the great pioneers of South Africa's freedom movement was M.K. Gandhi. India gave us M.K. Gandhi, we gave you back Mahatma Gandhi after two decades.'

Mahatma Gandhi was an apostle of non-violence. That is indeed the tradition of India—to enrich whichever nation we go, our foremost responsibility is to enrich that nation. Enriching the nation is not only in financial terms, but enrich with knowledge, enrich with sweat above all enrich with honour and self-dignity.

Dr Nelson Mandela when he became the President of South Africa gave the people who specialized in apartheid and ill-treated and put him in the jail, freedom to move, freedom to live in

South Africa as equal citizens. When Dr Nelson Mandela, or Madiba, as he was called in local language, passed away, he was given a burial with the presence of many heads of nations.

A big lesson that we learnt from Dr Nelson Mandela is beautifully captured in one of the *Thirukkurals* written 2,200 years ago by Thiruvalluvar:

It says for those who do ill to you, the best punishment
is to return good to them.

Two political leaders, Mahatma Gandhi and Dr Nelson Mandela, transformed India and South Africa into independent and democratic nations. This leadership has paved the way for many nations towards freedom.

I will now talk about Deng Xiaoping, the architect who saw the modern industrial revolution of China. Under his leadership, China acquired a rapidly growing economy, rising standards of living, and growing ties to the world economy. When Deng Xiaoping became pre-eminent leader of China in December 1978, China was still in the process of Cultural Revolution. By the time he stepped down in 1992, several hundred million Chinese citizens had been lifted out of poverty, and China was rapidly becoming stronger, richer and more modern.

To prepare for modernization Deng developed closer relations with the leading modern countries. He paved the way for closer relations with Europe, Japan and USA and various industrial nations. The economic vision of Deng Xiaoping for China is admired internationally.

Let me now share with you India's great visionary in space

science and technologies, Professor Vikram Sarabhai, who was my guru. Very rarely, in life's journey do great human beings influence us directly. I was fortunate to work with Professor Sarabhai for seven years. While working with him, I saw the dawn of the vision for the space programme in a one-page statement. Witnessing the evolution of this one page by many years of ceaseless work was really a great learning for me.

The famous vision statement of Professor Vikram Sarabhai made in the year 1970 states 'India with her mighty scientific knowledge and power house of young, should build her own huge rocket systems (satellite launch vehicles) and also build her own communication, remote sensing and meteorological spacecraft and launch from her own soil to enrich the Indian life in satellite communication, remote sensing and meteorology.' When I look at this vision statement now, I am overwhelmed to see the results of this statement. Today, India can build any type of satellite launch vehicle, any type of spacecraft and launch from Indian soil and also it has all the capability with its mighty facilities and powerful human resource. Through space technology and space science, India can be a partner in world space programme to enrich Earth and enable further exploration. I have seen myself how the international community in space is applauding Indian capabilities in bringing the benefits of this high technology to common people.

M.S. Swaminathan is known as the 'Father of the Green Revolution' in India for his leadership and success in introducing and further developing high-yielding varieties of wheat. Swaminathan chose agriculture as his field because of the Bengal

151

Famine of 1943, in which an estimated 3 million died. Greed exacted a terrible price in that famine, as people hoarded food until prices skyrocketed.

Swaminathan worked worldwide in collaboration with colleagues and students on a wide range of problems in basic and applied plant breeding, agricultural research and development and the conservation of natural resources. In 1983, he developed the concept of Farmers' Rights and the text of the International Undertaking on Plant Genetic Resources (IUPGR). He was elected president of the International Congress of Genetics. He received the first World Food Prize in October 1987. Swaminathan's relentless efforts created awareness that hunger is not a natural disaster but a disaster caused by human behaviour. Problems caused by human beings can always be solved by human beings. The first Green Revolution of India was pioneered by him with his team, guided by the political visionary Dr C. Subramaniam and supported by the farmers. They liberated India from the situation of what was called 'ship to mouth existence'. Through an effort of historical magnitude, India attained near self-sufficiency in food through 'seed to grain' mission. Of course, farmers played a pivotal role in working with agricultural scientists in making this happen.

Chandrasekhar Subramanyan's most famous discovery was the astrophysical Chandrasekhar limit. The limit describes the maximum mass (~1.44 solar masses) of a white dwarf star, or equivalently, the minimum mass for which a star will ultimately collapse into a neutron star or black hole following a supernova. The Chandrasekhar Limit led to the determination of how long a star of particular mass will shine. In 1983, Chandrasekhar Subramanyan got the Nobel Prize for this discovery

Two of Chandrasekhar's students in 1947 were the doctoral candidates Tsung-Dao Lee and Chen Ning Yang in particle physics research. Even though Chandrasekhar Subramanyan maintained his office at the Yerkes Observatory in Lake Geneva, Wisconsin, he would regularly drive the 100 miles to Chicago to guide and teach Lee and Yang and others many a times in difficult weather conditions. In 1957, these two of his students won the Nobel Prize in Physics for their work. His students got the Nobel prize three decades before he got it. This also brings out Chandrasekhar Subramanyan's commitment to science and to his students. Science indeed was a lifetime mission for Chandrasekhar. It is this characteristic which makes youth become passionate towards science.

Professor Satish Dhawan took over as Chairman, ISRO from Professor Sarabhai. A brilliant academician, and a shrewd technology manager, he created an institutional framework for Indian space research and development efforts interlinking the organization, industries, academic institutions and application users. He was instrumental in creating an organizational culture to manage development, projects, programmes and mission.

Finally, I will share with you a recent leadership success story. E. Sreedharan is popularly known as the 'Metro Man of India'. He served as the Managing Director of Delhi Metro between 1995-2012. In December 1964, a cyclone washed away parts of the Pamban Bridge that connected Rameswaram, my birth place, to mainland Tamil Nadu. The Railways set a target of three months for the bridge to be repaired. Sreedharan was put in charge of the execution and he restored the bridge in just forty-six days.

In 1970, Sreedharan was put in charge of implementation, planning and design of Calcutta Metro, the first ever metro in India. He was appointed the Chairman of Konkan Railways on contract in 1990. It was the first major project in India to be undertaken on a BOT (Build-Operate-Transfer) basis. The total project covered 760 km and had over 150 bridges and 93 tunnels through soft soil. That a public sector project could be completed without significant cost and time overruns was unprecedented in India. Sreedharan repeated the success story by creating the Delhi Metro by the target date or before, and within their respective budgets. He has emerged as a non-compromising perfectionist both on work standards, time frames and integrity in financial management. In 2005, he was awarded the Chevalier de la Légion d'honneur (Knight of the Legion of Honour) by the government of France.

So we see that:

a. Leader must be able to travel into an unexplored path.
b. Leader must know how to manage a success and failure.
c. Leader must have courage to take decisions.
d. Leader should have nobility in management.
e. Every action of the leader should be transparent.
f. Leader should work with integrity and succeed with integrity.

I have been discussing these essential traits of creative leaders with people of eminence in different areas and students from India and abroad. Apart from this what is needed is the spirit among the youth that I can do it, we can do it and the nation can do it. In an interconnected world, we may add the globe can do it also for the benefit of entire human kind. We have to concentrate on developing the leadership traits and the confidence to perform among the youth. This quality of leadership will certainly empower the people of the world.

(from Course on 'Sustainable Development System and Creative Leadership' Peking University, Beijing, 7 November 2014)

Healing with Heart

This is a great synergy between mind-body and medicine.

The medical profession has many dimensions. Let me begin with an experience with Choakyi Nyima Rinpoche, the chief monk in Kathmandu and a medical researcher. After nearly a kilometer of walk, I reached the white Kumbha where the chief monk and his disciples were waiting to receive me. After the reception the Rinpoche said, let us go to our study so I followed him. He climbed the first floor, the second floor, the third floor, the fourth floor and the fifth floor, as easily as a young boy. Probably his healthy lifestyle had a positive impact on the mind and body. All along I was following and following. When I reached his chamber, I saw it was a laboratory in a spiritual environment overlooking the Himalayas. What surprised me was his research students came from different parts of the world. He introduced me to his co-author David R. Shlim, MD. He has written with Dr David R. Shlim a book titled *Medicine and Compassion*. Choakyi Nyima Rinpoche and myself exchanged a few books. I liked their book and read it during my journey from Kathmandu to Delhi. This book gives six important virtues which a medical practitioner has to possess towards their patients:

- Generosity
- Pure ethics
- Tolerance

- Perseverance
- Cultivating pure concentration
- Be intelligent

These virtues will empower the caregivers with a humane heart. I am sure, those who wish to be doctors or are studying already to become doctors practice all these six virtues as a habit while dealing with patients. This is a great example of synergy between mind-body and medicine.

The world is facing a growing threat from new diseases that are jumping the human-animal species barrier as a result of environmental disruption, global warming and the progressive urbanisation of the planet. At least 45 diseases that have passed from animals to humans have been reported in the last two decades.

Science is an eternally evolving enterprise. It is a never-ending journey across generations of committed researchers. A good scientific institute, therefore, must be open to receive the new facts as they present themselves.

Healthcare professionals work with the philosophy 'what can I give'. I pray that you are empowered with new thoughts, renewed enthusiasm and commitment to your task. 'Let my brain remove the pain and bring well-being to the needy', must be the slogan. The global hospital at Mount Abu in partnership with two DRDO laboratories had worked for few years on the application of body-mind-soul synergy on allopathically treated cardiac patients. Scientifically, they have established that a three-dimensional solution definitely improves the condition of the patients and prevents recurrence of cardiac ailment in subsequent years. The three-dimensional solutions are: fibre rich vegetarian diet, aerobic exercises everyday and meditational practices.

A few years back, a friend of mine who is a scientist sent me a book *Biology of Beliefs* by Dr Bruce Lipton. The author is one of the greatest scientists of bio-science and after twenty years of research he has said the origin of human diseases and their cure have a basis in our intrinsic thinking and the relationship with our bio cells. The book talks about a new approach which highlights the importance of placebo effect and how it is actually a powerful belief. The author says, 'Doctors should not regard the power of belief as something inferior to the power of chemicals and scalpel. They should let go of the belief that the body and its parts are essentially stupid.'

Mahatma Gandhi has enumerated in one of his works, how thoughts lead to destiny. He said:

'Your beliefs become your thoughts
Your thoughts become your words
Your words become your actions
Your actions become your habits
Your habits become your values
Your values become your destiny.'

Let me now share a new medical invention with all of you.

Medical experts and engineers have taken a leaf out of nature's book by equipping an artificial hand with muscles. The new technology enables the fabrication of flexible and lightweight robot hands for industrial applications and novel prosthetic devices. The muscle fibres are composed of bundles of ultrafine nickel-titanium alloy wires that are able to tense and flex. The material itself has sensory properties allowing the artificial hand to perform extremely precise movements.

When I was in China, I visited the Peking University's centre for Robotics. There I met a number of experts working under Professor Li Michael Liu who showed me their new design for an adaptive prosthetic limb which responds to pressures and gradient change. I saw its demonstration and it gave mobility to those who had lost their leg. Professor told me that to make such a system he had to make a team of electrical engineers, medical specialist, rehab specialist and of course designers. Such is the integrated system where all work towards convergence of their knowledge.

Science thrives when it converges to solve pressing challenges of the world and this is the 21st century requirement from engineers. Whether we are in a developed country or developing country, there are certain common issues to be addressed particularly in healthcare sector, which include the following:

1. Affordable cost of healthcare without compromising on quality.
2. Preventive healthcare stressing on hygiene education, lifestyle care and upkeep of environment.
3. In a global world, nations cannot be just satisfied with good healthcare in specific localities or groups of the nation or the nation itself.
4. Shortage of clean water and energy can cause serious

healthcare problems.

5. There should be mechanisms to spread good deeds of medical practices and societal service from one part of the world to all over the globe.

6. Research and teaching are crucial aids to clinical practice and vice versa. There is a need to bring in worldwide knowledge platforms to find timely and cost effective solutions to healthcare issues.

Recently, there was a meeting of patients, their doctors and a few social workers. One important result was discussed. The relationship between the patient and doctor extends to the patients' family and doctor in medical care. This in turn, transmits effective messages from one family to another family on how to prevent diseases, the necessity of periodic checks, dietary habits and the need for lifestyle changes including exercises for good health. This good contact between the doctor and patients is comparable to that of a teacher and student. When you are a doctor, I request each one of you to play the role of a teacher in advising every family on disease prevention and methods to maintain quality health. I hope you all will find time for this noble action.

(from Address at Mysore Medical College and Research Institute, Mysore, 31 March 2015)